Salem Academy and College
FRIENDS of the LIBRARY

Gift of

The Friends of
the Library

TEXTUAL
CONFRON-
TATIONS

TEXTUAL CONFRON- TATIONS

Comparative Readings in
Latin American Literature

Alfred J. Mac Adam

The University of Chicago Press
Chicago and London

ALFRED J. MAC ADAM, professor of Spanish at Barnard College, is the author of *Modern Latin American Narratives: The Dreams of Reason*, also published by the University of Chicago Press.

The University of Chicago Press, Chicago 60637
The University of Chicago Press, Ltd., London
© 1987 by The University of Chicago
All rights reserved. Published 1987
Printed in the United States of America

96 95 94 93 92 91 90 89 88 87   5 4 3 2 1

Library of Congress Cataloging-in-Publication Data

Mac Adam, Alfred J., 1941–
　Textual confrontations.

　Bibliography: p.
　Includes index.
　Contents: Auden, Neruda, and Spain in 1937—
Countries of the mind, literary space in Joseph
Conrad and José Donoso—The novel of persecution,
from William Godwin to Reinaldo Arenas—Lewis
Carroll and Jorge Luis Borges—[etc.]
　　1. English literature—History and criticism.
　2. Latin American literature—History and criticism.
　3. Literature, Comparative—English and Latin American.
　4. Literature, Comparative—Latin American and English.
I. Title.
PR129.L38M33　1987　　860'.9'98　　86-24913
ISBN 0-226-49990-1

This book is dedicated to the memory of
Emir Rodríguez Monegal
and
John Lefebre

Contents

Preface

This collection of essays is an experiment in comparative literature. Its intention is modest: to juxtapose twentieth-century Latin American literary texts with works from the Anglo-American tradition. It is not absolutely historical; that is, while it does not ignore literary or social history, it does not seek to establish parallels or equivalencies between the literature of Latin America and that of Britain or the United States. Nor does it intend to establish equations between texts or movements: It simply wants to connect an eccentric branch of the Western tradition—Latin American literature—with British and American literature in order to reaffirm Latin America's place in that tradition and to explore those factors which render Latin American literature unique.

The selection of writers must inevitably seem arbitrary to the reader. There is no defense against such a charge except to say that the exercise of comparative literary criticism involves more than caprice. The connection might be a shared genre, a theme, two writers who come to grips with the same historical situation at exactly the same moment, or, conversely, two writers from different historical moments who try to deal with the same kind of historical dilemma. The unifying principle that reappears in all the essays is that Latin American literature belongs to the West, that it derives its identity from that tradition even as it stands in parodic relation to it.

These essays, then, are not comparison for comparison's sake or an exercise in literary legerdemain. They try to explain the changes that have taken place in Latin American literary history since the period of Spanish American Modernismo (roughly 1880–1920), when Spanish American writers attempted to bring their literary language and their writing up to date by imitating foreign, especially French, literature. The transformation that takes place in Latin American literature (that of both Spanish America and Brazil) after the twenties is that it goes from being a literature that tries to insinuate itself into the Western tradition by copying the reigning masters in Paris, to being a trendsetter in its own right.

It achieves this status by means of a special kind of imitation. Not the emulation carried out by the Modernistas, but parody, which it uses to turn the "lessons of the masters" upside down. Thus it gives back to what once were the centers of Western culture their own writing, now distorted and reshaped into something new.

At the same time, by reading "backward" from Latin American literature toward the Anglo-American tradition, we see as well that there is a fundamental diversity in that tradition, one invisible if we limit our reading to canonical texts. That is, by holding the Anglo-American tradition up to the parodic mirror of Latin American literature we see aspects of it that conventional literary history prefers to ignore.

Insofar as method is concerned, the essays collected here "let the punishment fit the crime." In other words, the critical approach seeks to be the one the texts themselves demand rather than any monolithic approach to all texts. The book reflects a personal obsession, the author's need to discuss Latin American and Anglo-American writing at the same time. In this sense, it is merely an attempt to inflict a personal madness on readers in the hope they see the method and purpose to it.

The author would like to take this opportunity to thank the following friends for their support during the years these essays were in gestation: Michael Seidel, Maria di Battista, James C. Nohrnberg, Paul H. Fry, Brigitte Peucker, Edward Mendelson, Alexander Coleman, and, of course, Barbara A. Mac Adam.

Early versions of these essays were given as lectures and symposium papers, but all have been substantially revised for this volume. A version of the Introduction appears in Alfred J. Mac Adam and Flora Schiminovich, "Latin American Literature in the Postmodern Era," in *The Postmodern Moment: A Handbook of Contemporary Innovation in the Arts,* ed. Stanley Trachtenberg (Westport, Conn.: Greenwood Press, 1985), pp. 251–62, copyright © 1985 by Stanley Trachtenberg; used by permission of the publisher.

Introduction

Comparative Literature and Latin American Literature

Comparative literature as a discipline has become something of a lost cause. It is wistfully cherished in the hearts of many and practiced in fact by only a few. Indeed, if comparative literature is the study of universal or general literature, the reasons why it has become a fading myth rather than a living reality are all too clear: Few literary scholars in the United States have the breadth of linguistic training—in the classical languages, French, German, Italian, Spanish, Portuguese, and at least one Oriental language—the discipline requires.

To study the development of the novel, for example, one would have to know these languages well enough not only to be able to read the "masterpieces" but the popular or commercial texts on which great novels are inevitably based, as Cervantes drew on the chivalric novel of the Middle Ages and the Renaissance and Flaubert on the sentimental romances of the nineteenth century. The sheer quantity of reading the ideal comparatist would have to do merely to be competent in the novel would require several lifetimes. Or, to put it another way: Let us imagine an individual interested in the novel who does not intend to devote his life to Balzac: How many novels of the *Comédie Humaine* constitute a "valid sample" of Balzac's production?

Even as they admit the impossibility of comparative

literary study as an absolute, René Wellek and Austin Warren argue persuasively for the comparative reading of literature:

Whatever the difficulties into which a conception of universal literary history may run, it is important to think of literature as a totality and to trace the growth and development of literature without regard to linguistic distinctions. The great argument for "comparative" or "general" literature or just "literature" is the obvious falsity of the idea of a self-enclosed national literature. Western literature, at least, forms a unity, a whole. One cannot doubt the continuity between Greek and Roman literatures, the Western medieval world, and the main modern literatures; and, without minimizing the importance of Oriental influences, especially that of the Bible, one must recognize a close unity which includes all Europe, Russia, the United States, and the Latin American literatures.[1]

Wellek and Warren tacitly confess that the literatures of China, Japan, India, Persia, and Arabia will certainly receive scant attention if comparative literature continues to be written from a Western point of view. In fact they recognize the convenience of doing exactly that: The "unities" they see in Western and Western-influenced areas (Latin America) makes literary study possible, especially when it is written according to the norms and forms literary history provides. The peripheral or marginal cultures of the West all hope to produce "their" Shakespeare or "their" Flaubert.

The problem is that the homogeneity of Western culture is breaking down. Not only do we possess histories of "exotic" literatures—a parallel to the West's acquisition of the art of other cultures, which it stores in museums—but we possess as well the peoples of those other cultures. Their physical presence will inevitably contribute to the breakdown of all barriers between Western and non-Western literary study. As we become more cosmopolitan we will find more and more literary possibilities open to us.

A great deal will doubtless be lost in the process: The blending of cultures will engender a homogenization, a loss of individual traits. The first of these losses will no doubt be language. Immigrants tend to adopt the language of the countries in which they settle. That loss has a parallel in the United States in the decline of language study: Knowing a "foreign" language is no longer required by many American universities. And "computer languages" are actually considered more important for some disciplines than human languages. Against this trend toward monolingualism is the fact that those who do wish training in foreign languages may now travel with relative ease to the lands where those languages are spoken. (Or not travel at all, if the "foreign" language happens to be Spanish, since so many citizens of the United States speak only Spanish.)

Another problem at least as crucial as language learning is literary study itself. As the visual media come to occupy more and more space in our culture, the literary tradition finds itself threatened. Today's undergraduates balk at reading long novels, probably because their attention span is conditioned by television, and literary history is such a forgotten science that it is difficult to find an undergraduate who understands the notion of historical difference. In this sense, the study of comparative literature, the actual juxtaposition of literary works from disparate cultures and languages, even if these are safely within the cultural unity Wellek and Warren see in Western society, is both anachronistic and utopian. It asks readers to open their eyes to new perspectives at a moment when those same readers are losing touch with their own literary tradition.

The essays in this volume cannot resolve the problem of cultural decline. They can, however, address the aesthetic question of just what shape comparative literary study should take. At every turn, the comparatist runs into the problem of universals. For example, the poetic forms the West takes for granted, odes or elegies let's say, may have no equivalent in Indian literature. Similarly, while translations of Chinese novels have been delighting Western readers for decades, can we say that the novel in China has had the same cultural value it has had in the West? Are we sure we know what the aesthetic and cultural intentions of the novel are in our own culture? The same problems apply to comparative literary history: Unless we create for literature those ingenious comparative charts that tell us that while gunpowder was being invented in China some form of compass was being used in Ireland—surrealistic exercises that fascinate us with their juxtapositions even if they are ultimately meaningless— we impose our literary history on other cultures. We suddenly find ourselves moving from a cultural fact, Romanticism for example, to a metaphor: "This period in Japanese literature corresponds to our Romantic period."

This domestication of the exotic demonstrates just how inadequate the tools we use to understand our own literature are, especially our ideas of literary history. In "Towards Literary History," Geoffrey Hartman criticizes literary history and tells why something must be done to change it:

We are all disenchanted with those picaresque adventures in pseudo-causality which go under the name of literary history, those handbooks with footnotes which claim to sing of the whole but load every rift with glue. . . . [I]f I raise the question of literary history, it is not merely to urge its importance as an intellectual discipline or to deplore the absence of

methodological thinking in that area. . . . My argument will be that literary history is necessary less for
the sake of intellect than for the sake of literature—it
is our historical duty because it alone can provide
today a sorely needed defense of art.[2]

In the same essay, Hartman suggests we turn to the
artists themselves to discover some working hypoth-
eses for a new literary history. He finds a model in the
principle of conflict:

No great writer is without an identity crisis. The
shape of that crisis can be generalized. Though we
may not always discern what developmental impasse
occurs within the poet's private life, we can describe
the vocational crisis that occurs in the poet as poet, in
his literary self-consciousness. A great artist has the
ambition to seize (and hand on) the flame of inspiration, to identify the genius of art with his own genius
or that of a particular age (genius loci). (p.367)

Harold Bloom, in his highly influential *The Anxiety of
Influence: A Theory of Poetry*,[3] also denounces as false
the idea we find in T. S. Eliot's "Tradition and the
Individual Talent" (1919), namely that to write poetry
is to escape from individual personality. Hartman and
Bloom remain squarely in the ranks of the post-
Romantic tradition, which extols the individual. As
Hartman says: "The artist's struggle with his vocation—with past masters and the "pastness" of art in
modern society—seems to be a version of a universal
struggle: of genius with Genius, and of genius with the
genius loci (spirit of the place) (p.372). It is the guiding
principle of his approach to literary history, and may
stand as a means whereby readers may understand the
conflictive relationship between Latin American literature and the literature of the metropolitan cultures of
the Western world.

Claudio Guillén[4] has taken this idea of struggle and

applied it to literary genres: Each genre constitutes not only an independent literary form but a conflictive relationship between genres. For Guillén, *Don Quijote* is "an inspired response to the challenge of the new-born picaresque genre" (p.146), and the "negative impacts or influences *à rebours,* through which a norm is dialectically surpassed (and assimilated) by another, or a genre by a countergenre, constitute one of the main ways in which a literary model acts upon a writer" (pp.146–47). This "challenge-and-response" understanding of the relationship between literary genres deflects our attention away from the artists-in-conflict principle of Hartman and Bloom and makes us concentrate on the literary text in the world of readers and in the company of other literary texts. In this way, it demands we take the historical moment in which the text appears into account: We must know who its readers are (especially other writers) and which genres it is either attempting to overcome or to imitate.

Northrop Frye[5] postulates a different theory of the relationship among literary genres: His is not based on conflict but on the relationship each genre has to a specific *Weltanschauung.* Frye locates literary genres on a vast, segmented wheel; each segment corresponds to one of the seasons, which are ultimately the seasons of human life and the phases in the life of a state or people. Tragedy is related to winter, to eschatology, end things, death, and decay, while comedy reflects summer, life, and fecundity. Frye does not suggest that authors necessarily produce tragedies when societies are on the verge of dissolution, or that triumphant societies only entertain themselves with comedies. For Frye, the genres embody an idealized or idiosyncratic vision of society at a given moment. An author may choose among options or even create new ones through irony. Shakespeare wrote comedies and tragedies, but wrote something that was neither and yet both when he composed *Measure for Measure,* an ironic comedy in which the fixtures of comedy are present but with their emblems of fertility and joy curiously inverted.

Frye envisions the relationship among literary genres as a vast *ars combinatoria* where authors infinitely recombine, according to their fancy, already extant forms. The novel, for example, grows out of history writing combined with a parody of romance. The Latin American fiction of the sixties, following Frye, is to a great extent a parodic, satiric inversion of the novel, romance, and history, a bizarre yet totally Western concept of literature as an author's reassessment of his personal relationship to tradition as well as the relationship of his national culture to the dominant cultures of the West. Among contemporary speculations on the question of literary genres, Frye's is the most organically complete and critically satisfying because it takes into account factors most theories of literature have difficulty treating, namely literary change, irony, and the historicity of genres.

The recent translation and diffusion of the critical writings of Mikhail Bakhtin provides yet another vision of literary genres, one that modifies but in no way negates Frye's. Among the ideas on genre Bakhtin presented over the course of his career, two are particularly relevant to the comparative study of Latin American and Anglo-American literature: first, the concept of generic memory (*Problems of Dostoevsky's Poetics*).[6] A genre contains within it, as it were, the entire genetic code for that specific genre; that is, while a given text participates in the historical moment in which it is written and read, it also participates in the history of the genre itself by recapitulating those distinctive features that identify the genre. Identifying these traits is all-important in a reading of Latin American literature, precisely because while the Latin American cultural-historical tradition is often broken or nonexistent as a historical continuum, the connection between present and past exists because of the genre's own historical continuity.

The second concept Bakhtin contributes to our understanding of genre in the Latin American context is the relationship between genres and historical contingency. An author has available to him at the moment of writing a number of generic options: Which one he chooses, which ones he parodies, which ones he disregards completely, which ones he cannot practice—these are the links between the individual artist and his immediate historical situation and his literary tradition, as he feels it. To move from that point to the study of the genre itself is, again, to study the text both in its local context and in the stream of literary tradition.

But the vision of literary production as struggle, extending Hartman and Bloom beyond poetry, takes on special importance when we deal with Latin America, whose relationship to Western culture is not as harmonic as Wellek and Warren suggest. The "close unity" they see among Europe, Russia, the United States, and Latin America, the result of education, religion, language, and history, actually produces more diversity than cohesion. The "belatedness" of colonial cultures—the term appears in an essay by Ernst Robert Curtius on Spain[7]—has become something of an irony, especially since the 1960s. The idea of a center of Western culture, a "Paris, Capital of the Nineteenth Century," in Walter Benjamin's sense,[8] is either an anachronism or a nostalgia. As economic hegemony in the West passed after World War II to the United States, the cultural domination of the Western world by any of the European states faded. The United States assumed an important role in Western cultural life but did so in a rather chaotic fashion.

Unlike France or England, the United States does not

concentrate its cultural, political, and economic centers in one place. There are many centers spread over a vast space in a country that has traditionally resisted the centralization of power. The large number of state and private universities together with the paradoxical absence of any national university also contributes to the diffusion of culture. Local schools of all kinds crop up—the Chicago economists and the Chicago Aristotelian critics are examples—but they tend to be ephemeral and their disciples scatter over the land. It is, therefore, difficult to single out a predominant tendency in any aspect of cultural life in the United States; and to speak of anything beyond general tendencies in the plastic arts, literature, or dance is impossible. The exceptions always outnumber the rule, a fact that engenders among academics and artists a nostalgia for vanished centers.

Paris in the 1980s is not the cultural center of the Western world, as it was throughout the nineteenth and the early twentieth century, but it still retains its prestige for Latin American writers. Like the Spanish American Modernistas of the last century, Latin American writers and artists still make their sentimental pilgrimage to Paris, some, like Julio Cortázar and Severo Sarduy, to become permanent residents. While New York and other American cities have replaced it during the eighties, Paris was still the international capital of Latin America during the sixties. The literary magazine that introduced the "new Latin American narrative" to the Spanish-speaking world, *Mundo Nuevo*, edited by Emir Rodríguez Monegal from 1966 until 1968,[9] had its offices in Paris. And the participation of so many Latin American intellectuals in UNESCO, directed by the Mexican poet Jaime Torres Bodet from 1948 to 1952, also brought a large Latin American contingent to the French capital. Paris, to echo Horacio Oliveira, the expatriate Argentine protagonist of Julio Cortázar's *Hopscotch* (1963), was an "enormous metaphor," one that stood for a lost center that probably never existed in reality.

Literary critics also suffer from nostalgia, although Paris in this instance is innocent of any complicity in it. This is a longing for absolute meaning in literary texts, something much modern literary criticism and theory have called into question. To restore the idea of meaning to literature, critics have sought to reduce literary history to a subspecies of cultural history or history of ideas and to explain literary phenomena in terms of social or political history. This kind of critical thinking is ultimately ideological and takes on two general forms. One would be the type practiced by Hernán Vidal in his *Literatura hispanoamericana e ideologia liberal: surgimiento y crisis.*[10] Vidal discovers that the Boom—the "new Latin American novel" of the sixties—reflects mass-marketing techniques applied to literature, that both the Boom and its critics are committed to capitalism as applied to cultural enterprises. He uses these conclusions to launch an attack on the bourgeois ideology of certain writers and to indict the Boom and "formalist" criticism. He concludes his essay with a meditation on Julio Cortázar, who, in a 1970 discussion that took place in Paris between artists and critics from Latin America and students, found himself alienated from the young people in the audience who questioned the ideology of his writing. Vidal, writing six years after the confrontation, sees in it the moment when Cortázar begins to acquire a more "committed" ideological attitude, a moment when he ceases to be an alienated, bourgeois writer, one Cortázar himself envisioned (using images from Verlaine) as a Roman of the Decadence surrounded by barbarians. Vidal sees another image of Cortázar and Latin American writers in general arising at that moment:

another more concrete, more human archetype of the writer: one who does not conceive of himself as a being split between body and soul, but a writer who instead combines the two in revolutionary praxis and thinks of himself as just one more cultural worker. In the meantime, the narrative of the Boom has become the pitiable spectacle of writers—and critics—who seek to shed their liberal, petit-bourgeois skin, even as others who have already exhausted their powers in this struggle slowly join the ranks of the reactionaries. (p.112; my trans.)

This certainly separates the sheep from the goats. For Vidal, a writer is either one of the blessed (ideologically correct, revolutionary) or one of the damned (ideologically incorrect, bourgeois, reactionary). This political vision of culture provides as well a hierarchy of literary values and a method for literary evaluation.

That the Boom of the late sixties reflected an attempt to apply modern marketing techniques to the Latin American novel is certainly true, but there is one aspect of it that eludes Vidal's analysis. From his essay, it would seem that a group of writers appeared out of nowhere, that the publishers somehow conjured them into existence, and that the same magical mechanism created readers for these writers. Even a cursory examination of the writers of the sixties demonstrates a level of sophistication that can only come about when a literature has had time to mature and has a readership that has also had a chance to reach the same level of familiarity with literary technique. Julio Cortázar, Gabriel Garcia Márquez, Manuel Puig, José Donoso, and Mario Vargas Llosa (to name a few Boom writers) were "best-sellers" within Spanish America long before their international success. What the commercial side of the Boom accomplished was to make them international best-sellers in a Spanish American and Latin American context, to break the parochial narrowness that had kept Mexican readers from taking Peruvian or Argentine writers seriously.

But even slick marketing cannot explain the quality of the writing the Boom produced. That writing, too, did not spring fully grown from the mind of a literary agent or publishing-house owner. It was the result of generations of writers toiling to convince a reading public—a small, but in general well-educated reading public—that it should take literature "made in Latin America" seriously and not read only European or North American writing. The most outstanding example of the pre-Boom writer would have to be Jorge Luis Borges, whose extraordinary short story collections, *Ficciones* and *El Aleph* were published in the forties. As artist, critic, and translator (of Kafka, Faulkner, and Virginia Woolf), Borges helped shape the minds of readers, precisely those who would later read Cortázar and Donoso.

To say that this is an elitist literature, of the bourgeoisie, by the bourgeoisie, and for the bourgeoisie, is correct but misleading. Of course, one might ask who in fact would write if not that thin literate stratum present in most Latin American countries, just as one might similarly ask who would read, if not those same people. To condemn that writing (and, by the same token, those readers) is to discard some of the finest artistic productions of the twentieth century—for ideological reasons. A bizarre notion, but one that is common in the twentieth century whenever politics meddles with literature.

The second ideologically motivated type of criticism is that typified by John Gledson's *The Deceptive Realism of Machado de Assis: A Dissenting Interpretation of 'Dom Casmurro.'*[11] For Gledson, "realism" is not a literary style or movement as practiced by Flaubert or Galdós but a value. A literary work of art is good if it can be demonstrated to be "realistic," which means to be a kind of history writing with imaginative touches:

Here I wish to start from the premise that what Machado's novels set out to do is in essence no different from what many nineteenth- (and seventeenth-, eighteenth- and twentieth-) century novels try to do, that is, to give us a view of the society to which the novelist belongs. (p.2)

So much for literature as entertainment or as the work of imagination. So much, in fact, for art. What Gledson seeks to do in his study of Machado de Assis is to bring about Wellek and Warren's "close unity" of Western culture by an act of violence: He attempts to domesticate Latin American culture by showing that it is nothing more than a slightly modified form of Western culture. Machado de Assis is as much a realist as Flaubert—formalist critics just haven't been reading him correctly. The ideological aspect of this literary homogenization process is that realism for Gledson is actually the only ideologically acceptable form of writing. It is not only that Machado de Assis is a realist, it is that critics who use other literary approaches to his work are essentially perverting it. Thus, Gledson wants to save Machado de Assis from the critics, while Hernán Vidal would condemn both the writing and the critics.

These history-bound critics keep alive the spirit (if not the ideology) of Hippolyte Taine and make no statements about literature that cannot be either verified or justified by allusion to historical sources. Thus they render literature the effect of historical causes. Their dependence on history as the ultimate authority in literary matters renders any forays they might make into comparative literature timid at best. In fact, they virtually reject comparative literary study and encapsulate whatever literature they study within national, regional, or linguistic boundaries, unless, as in Gledson's manipulation of the concept of literary realism, allusion to other cultures suits their ideological purposes.

To follow such a program with regard to Latin American literature is simply impossible. It flies in the face of Latin American reality, which, since the Renaissance, has been one of cultural and economic dependence coupled with intellectual eccentricity, a common element that links such disparate figures from pre-twentieth-century Spanish America as El Inca Garcilaso de la Vega (1539–1616), Sor Juana Inés de la Cruz (1651–95), and Fray Servando Teresa de Mier (1765–1827). Thus, Latin American writers have always felt a need to be part of their national or regional culture and to participate in the larger Western tradition at the same time. Carlos Fuentes succinctly defines this situation:

One of the basic cultural factors of Latin America is that it is an eccentric branch of the culture of the West. It is Western and it is not Western. So we feel that we have to know the culture of the West even better than a Frenchman or an Englishman, and at the same time we have to know our own culture. This sometimes means going back to the Indian cultures, whereas the Europeans feel they don't have to know our cultures at all. We have to know Quetzalcoatl *and* Descartes. They think Descartes is enough. So Latin America is a constant reminder to Europe of the duties of its universality. Therefore, a writer like Borges is a typically Latin American writer. The fact that he is so European only indicates that he is Argentinian. No European would feel obliged to go to the extremes Borges does to create a reality, not to mirror a reality but to create a new reality to fill in the cultural voids of his own tradition.[12]

Fuentes's statement naturally obliges us to consider the reader of Latin American fiction, to take up the matter of the reception of Latin American literature by Latin American and non–Latin American readers. Wolfgang Iser[13] and Hans Robert Jauss[14] have recast traditional literary history to take into account the reader as not merely the consumer of literature but as producer of literary meaning. Their efforts derive in part from their cultural milieu: They seek to blaze a path between the Scylla of Marxist aesthetics, which tends to be prescriptive and limiting, and the Charybdis of formalism, which does not deal with literature in a historical context. Each in his own way hopes to recover the historical impact of individual texts, either through a reconstruction of the readership or through a reading of the text that would isolate the cues the text provides about how it wants to be read. This latter idea, the more feasible of the two projects, is one of the more exciting contemporary critical programs because it attempts to make the reader aware of the literary work of art as a multifaceted totality that includes instructions for use. This idea appears as well in E. D. Hirsch's discussion of "instrinsic genres" in *Validity in Interpretation*,[15] where he declares that if the reader is unaware of the text's generic signals, he will read the text improperly.

Taking the reader into account, both the reader who was the author's original audience and the reader in the abstract sense of anyone who might be attuned to the text's suggestions about reading, reminds us of the dynamic nature of literary history and of the many ironies inherent in the reading process. In fact, it was Jorge Luis Borges who first dramatized the role of the reader, in stories such as "Pierre Menard, Author of the *Quijote*," and "Averroes's Search," and his seminal essay "The Homeric Versions" (1932). The fragments of *Don Quijote* that Pierre Menard, a late, provincial Symbolist, manages to write, while textually identical to Cervantes's original, mean something totally different. They "mean" what Menard's age, given its beliefs and biases, would have them mean. Similarly, Averroes, the medieval Hispano-Arabic translator and explicator of Aristotle, reaches an impasse when he comes to the *Poetics:* How can he comprehend tragedy when he has never seen a play or been in a theater? "The Homeric Versions" examines the translations (for Borges translation is always a species of reading, itself a metaphor for writing) of Homer into English. He asks if any translation is superior to any other and concludes that each age reads Homer according to its own lights and remakes him in its own image.

Borges, as he does so often, cautions us about the ironies attendant on such ideas as authorial intention and textual meaning. To have an impact on a tradition or a reader, a text must be assimilated by an audience. And how it is absorbed produces the ambiguities that constitute the "meaning" of the text. Mikhail Bakhtin describes this process in temporal terms:

Before us are two events—the event that is narrated in the work and the event of narration itself (we ourselves participate in the latter, as listeners or readers); these events take place in different times (which are marked by different durations as well) and in different places, but at the same time these two events are indissolubly united in a single but complex event that we might call the work in the totality of all its events, including the external material givenness of the work, and its text, and the world represented in the text, and the author-creator and the listener or reader; thus we perceive the fullness of the work in all its wholeness and indivisibility, but at the same time we understand the diversity of the elements that constitute it.[16]

Each reader, each reading, reconstitutes "the work in the totality of all its events," but each is different. Here we see that Wellek and Warren's "close unity" of Western civilization is a pious fiction. If we give names to the figures in Bakhtin's description of the reading process, if, for example, we imagine Rubén Dario, the outstanding Spanish American poet of the late nineteenth century, born in Nicaragua in 1867, reading Mallarmé, we wonder just what Bakhtin's "work in the totality of all its events" might be. Certainly it would be markedly different, although we cannot be sure about the details, from a reading by Yeats (born in 1865) or Valéry (born in 1871). To what extent is any reading of a text by someone not from the author's immediate historic, linguistic, and social context a parody? Here again we might recall Borges's story about Averroes trying to write a commentary on Aristotle's *Poetics* without ever having seen a play or a stage.

We must expand the notion of parody to include not only an author's deliberate misrepresentations but those unconsciously wrought by the reader. The fear of incurring these involuntary parodies has always made Latin American writers sensitive to the differences between the cultures in which they live and the "other" culture, that of the metropolitan centers, real or imagined, of the Western world. In this they are different from their counterparts in the United States, at least in the twentieth century, who imagine the Anglo-American tradition to be self-sufficient. And no doubt the fact that the independence of the United States did not mean a break with the burgeoning literary world of Great Britain in the late eighteenth and nineteenth centuries is an important factor in this sense of continuity, which contrasts sharply with the separation of Spanish America from a Spain that in the early nineteenth century was still in the throes of the cultural decline that had begun at the end of the seventeenth century.

Latin American culture, because of political and economic instability, constantly reminds itself of its own insufficiency. Carlos Fuentes's observation about the

Latin American writer's having one foot firmly planted in local culture and the other in cosmopolitan culture has engendered in recent years a strange kind of literary history. Ideologically inspired critics in the line of Hernán Vidal and John Gledson divide authors into those who mirror reality faithfully and those who turn their backs on their reality. These latter they define as "inauthentic" Latin American writers. The list of inauthentic writers includes many of the late nineteenth-century Modernistas (who renovated the literary language of the Spanish-speaking world) and Borges, even though each of the books he published between 1923 and 1932 deals with Argentina. The purging of these writers from the Spanish American canon means, as in the case of the Boom, purging the best of Latin American writing for purely ideological reasons.

Another result of this political reading of Latin American culture is the denial of the hybrid nature of that culture. Once that fact only served as an index of Latin America's belatedness, but now it demonstrates its vitality. That vigor derives precisely from misreading, in a way both willful and accidental, Latin America's parodic relationship with the Western tradition.

Within Latin America itself, the enigma of that culture's true identity has spawned a polemic we may loosely call "the Caliban controversy." The history of this polemic, which has been summarized by Emir Rodríguez Monegal,[17] begins with the Uruguayan man of letters José Enrique Rodó (1871–1917), who attempted, in his essay *Ariel* (1900), to forge a myth that would restore Spanish American self-esteem in the dark days after the Spanish American war of 1898. That war not only signaled the end of Spain's empire in the New World but pointed out the growing hegemony of the United States in the New World.

Rodó, more influenced by Ernest Renan's play *Caliban* (1878) than by Shakespeare, urged Latin Americans to identify their culture with the figure of Ariel, the airy spirit who for Rodó symbolized the refined and the ideal, and to associate the United States with Caliban, the materialistic, the utilitarian, and the ugly. In Renan, Caliban leaves his island, comes to France, and becomes a demagogue—a symbol of the dangers of democracy, when the mob is given political power. Rodó, a conservative, also feared total democracy, which for him could mean only the anarchy that had plagued Uruguay and much of Spanish America throughout the nineteenth century. In effect, Rodó translates Renan's antidemocratic thought into a desire for stability.

Rodó was fully aware that his essay was myth-making, but later generations of Spanish American cultural critics, Roberto Fernández Retamar notable among them,[18] have not treated him charitably, charging that he was blind to the realities of Latin America. The charge is unfair, but it does mark an important phenomenon, the inversion of Rodó's myth of Latin America as Ariel. Latin Americans have come increasingly to see themselves as Caliban, the cannibal, the exploited native of the island Prospero (the United States) conquers. The idea that Caliban is the first mestizo in literature, possibly the product of the union between Prospero and the witch Sycorax, as *The Tempest* itself suggests when Prospero ambiguously remarks about Caliban, "This thing of darkness I acknowledge mine" (V,1,275), also heightens the identification.

That Latin America is the result of cultural *mestizaje*—and that the "Latin" element is no more important than the Indian or African element—is an undeniable fact, one that Latin Americans, especially during the nineteenth century, when positivist race theories were in vogue, considered a handicap. This repression of the non-European side of Latin America continued until the Brazilian Modernistas founded their *Revista de Antropofagia* (1928–29). They declared that their relationship to the West was and would be cannibalistic: They would ingest Western culture and make it into something new by fusing it with their own being.

The result is parody. Bakhtin describes the stages in literary production that lead to parody by beginning with "stylization," "an artistic representation of another's linguistic style, an artistic image of another's language" (p.362). Parody is different from stylization because

the intentions of the representing discourse are at odds with the intentions of the represented discourse; they fight against them, they depict a real world of objects not by using the represented language as a productive point of view, but rather by using it as an exposé to destroy the represented language. This is the nature of *parodic stylization. (Dialogic Imagination*, p.364)

If we were to use Bakhtin's notions of stylization and parody as an approach to Spanish American literary history, expanding it to include poetry as well as prose, we could say that the late nineteenth century and the early twentieth century (from 1880 to 1920), the period of Spanish American Modernismo, was a time of stylization, while the period since 1920 has been marked by a tendency toward parody. If we understand Modernismo as an attempt to bring the literary language of the Spanish-speaking world up to date by incorporating into it the literary languages of other nations, France especially, we see why it was a conscious effort at stylization and why it would ultimately arouse the xenophobic wrath of later literary generations.

That Modernismo entailed stylization does not automatically mean that it produced derivative or inferior literature. This privileging of originality is a Romantic prejudice of no particular validity, but stylization, the incorporation of alien literary techniques into one's literary culture, is no guarantee of literary success. Modernismo was more successful in certain areas, lyric poetry, for example, than it was in others—in particular the novel.

Even after 1920, the Spanish American novel is weak in comparison with the lyric, especially with such strong poets as Pablo Neruda and César Vallejo on the literary scene. There are many explanations for this weakness in narrative, ranging from a dearth of novel-readers to the theory that the Hispanic genius expresses itself best in verse. There may well be some truth (or half-truth) in these ideas, but they do not take into account the kind of novel actually being produced in Spanish America in the late nineteenth and early twentieth century: It too is a stylization, an appropriation of some other culture's literary style used to represent (since it aspired to realism) Spanish American reality. The problem was that the devices of Realism and Naturalism were not suited to the recreation of Spanish American reality, and the result, with some exceptions, was a mass of well-intentioned but derivative texts, books whose models were all too clear.

In Brazil, however, the transition from stylization to parody took place during the period of Spanish American Modernismo. A radically different kind of prose fiction appeared when Joaquim Maria Machado de Assis (1839–1908) published *As Memórias Póstumas de Brás Cubas* in 1880: the modern Latin American satiric novel was born. Flying in the face of Realism, Machado chose fantasy: His novel is narrated by a dead man. Machado's use of the fantastic, together with his decision to reduce character to stereotype and to present society as a madhouse set him apart from his Latin American contemporaries.

Why Machado should have written in this vein is one of the mysteries of literary history, but one to

which literary history may provide at least a provision-
al solution. Machado the reader seems to have found
the English eighteenth-century novel, particularly
Tristram Shandy, more congenial as material for stylization than, say, the novels of Flaubert. In the satiric
novel he found a structure he could adapt to a representation of Brazilian reality with more success than he
would have had if he had attempted to rewrite
Madame Bovary in a Brazilian setting. Which is not to
say that Flaubert did not influence Machado: He did at
the level of theme, but he did not at the level of character and novelistic structure.

Machado invents modern Latin American narrative
by, paradoxically, being old-fashioned. Anachronism is
as much a part of modern Latin American fiction as
parody, and Machado may be said to have discovered
that there is no evolution or progress in literature. To
write in an eighteenth-century mode at the height of
the Realist period was simultaneously to deny the
modern as such and to satirize contemporary literary
conventions.

Brás Cubas is a stylization of Sterne used to create a
caricature of nineteenth-century Brazilian life. Its style
derives from eighteenth-century models and its structure certainly derives from *Tristram Shandy*. The English novelists of the nineteenth century, particularly
Thackeray and Dickens, also show the lasting influence of eighteenth-century satire: We see it when
Thackeray refers to his characters as puppets at the end
of *Vanity Fair* and when Dickens uses transparently
satiric names—Smallweed or Guppy for example—for
his characters. It was that same tendency toward social
satire and caricature that attracted Machado and
moved him away from the psychological realism of the
French novel, the feeling we have when reading
Dickens, that fairy-tale and romance are hovering just
on the fringes of his writing. The mixture of fantasy

(from the preter- to the super-natural) and satiric stylization is the hallmark of the Latin American narrative
of our own century, a truly Calibanesque writing that
stands the immediate tradition of Realism on its head.

Why the mechanisms of Realism were not suitable
for the representation of Latin American life, why the
novel took so long to develop in Latin America are
problems for which literary history offers no real solutions. The transition from stylization to parody, our
adaptation of Bakhtin's terms, which constitute no
progression of any kind in his essay, is nothing more
than an explanatory metaphor, one that seeks to connect two phases of Latin American literary production
while retaining the idea that this production is closely
related to the way in which Latin American writers
read the literature of the Western world. The phase of
stylization views cosmopolitan literature as a source of
models to imitate and acclimate to the Latin American
milieu, while the phase of parody sees Western literary
texts as raw material to be absorbed and transformed
into something new. Something quite strange for both
Latin American and non–Latin American readers. This
is, clearly, the inversion of the colonial economic system where, traditionally, the colonies supply the metropolis with raw material which the metropolis turns
into manufactured goods to resell (at a profit) to the
colonies.

The origin of this inversion, leaving aside the unique
case of Machado de Assis (himself an argument in favor
of artistic genius overcoming social, political, economic, and aesthetic limitations), is history itself, the
legacy of World War I and Oswald Spengler's seminal
book *The Decline of the West* (1918). The spectacle of
the war that brought France, England, Germany, and
Russia to the brink of disaster, together with Spengler's
theory about the life-cycle that all cultures have, made
Latin America turn its back—or pretend to turn its

back—on Europe and look for cultural myths within itself. The decline of Europe (the title of Spengler's book in the Russian translation) was an all-pervading axiom in the twenties and was circulated in Latin America by José Ortega y Gasset in essays on Spengler he published in his ironically titled magazine *Revista de Occidente.* The effect, both of the general principle of European decline and of Spengler's book (published in Spanish in 1923), appears in the writings of the young Borges, who read Spengler in German and wrote about him during the twenties and thirties. It was during those decades that Borges sought to formulate an aesthetic program that would be non-European and consonant with what he thought best in Argentine culture, the semibarbarous *criollo.*[19]

The totally Europeanized Borges of 1925 could never purge himself of a European culture that was part of his very essence, but his search for a "native" aesthetics is symptomatic of Latin America's changing relationship with the West. Borges's search—and we must remember that the Borges of the twenties was a poet-essayist, not a writer of prose fiction—for a truly Argentine literary language was a means whereby he could declare his own independence from Europe and attack the Spanish American Modernistas, particularly Rubén Darío, for being the apes of decadent European Symbolism. Borges's rejection of Darío's stylization of Parnassian and Symbolist poetry is his first step toward parody and is characteristic of the destructive early twentieth-century Latin American avant-garde. Even as they attack Darío and a Europe they define as bankrupt, they use the devices the European avant-garde employs to liberate itself from its immediate cultural past.

This technique of attacking Europe in order to assert personal aesthetic freedom becomes a tradition in Latin America. In 1949, the Cuban Alejo Carpentier rather belatedly repeats the Spenglerian assault on Europe in the preface[20] to his novella *El reino do este mundo* (*The Kingdom of This World*). Carpentier goes further than Borges in that he rejects the European avant-garde as well as most European literature since the Gothic novel and Romanticism. His claim is that European literature tries to create supernatural effects for readers who do not believe in the supernatural and that such prestidigitation is merely artificial. The Americas, Carpentier argues, need no such artificiality because they are imbued with what he calls a "real marvelous" ("real maravilloso"). No matter how self-deceptive such an act of cultural self-assertion may appear—Carpentier's discovery of the Americas' "real marvelous" is no more (or less) fanciful than Rodó's identification of Latin America with Ariel in 1900—it is necessary in the parodic phase of Latin American literature because it allows the writer to project an independent self-image, one that allows him to delineate his own literary space.

That space is made up of words, a style that identifies the individual writer by revealing both what he is and what he is not. But literary language in the parodic phase of Latin American literature comes into being as the result of the writer's ironic awareness of the dual nature of Latin American culture. He realizes it is an unstable compound of local and foreign elements, mixed and clashing. For Latin American prose fiction, which has eclipsed poetry since the sixties, this realization has produced a "hybridization." Bakhtin declares that hybridization is essential to literary prose, especially to the novel:

the novelistic hybrid is an *artistically organized system for bringing different languages in contact with one another*, a system having as its goal the illumination of one language by means of another, the carving-out of a living image of another language. (*Dialogic Imagination*, p. 361)

Hybridization in the Latin American context has produced texts that are galleries of literary voices rather than transcriptions of reality. Following Borges's aesthetic lead, writers have come to the paradoxical conclusion that language is their only reality although, at the same time, that reality is as illusory as any other. That is, the Latin American novelist has become acutely aware of his own language in all its permutations: the spoken language (at all social and aesthetic levels), the written language (at all social and aesthetic levels), and the relation of that language to external languages, the spoken and written languages of the West. The result is a baroque intermingling of forms of discourse, a literary language that is simultaneously local and cosmopolitan, a reflection of specific times and places and a stylization.

This self-conscious stance typifies the parodic literature of Latin America. In a sense, it recalls Milton's attitude toward the Renaissance. Milton, an artist of baroque sensibility, feels obliged to include all the tropes, all the devices, not only of the classical epics but of all the Renaissance epics into *Paradise Lost*. At the same time, he is impelled to show his knowledge of contemporary science. He feels a literary *horror vacui* and the result is an intellectually overloaded text. The same is true for many Latin American writers: They know a great deal and require their readers to know at least as much. They construct encyclopedic books, texts that are pedagogic as well as aesthetic enterprises. This is a risky business in a world where illiteracy is rampant and where politcally oriented critics charge them with elitism. But such a literature is not created in a vacuum. There has existed, at least until the Latin American economic and political debacle of the seventies, which has threatened to disrupt the educational system of many countries, a small but well-educated public for this neobaroque Latin American literature throughout Latin America. The future of this readership is one of the ambiguities of contemporary Latin American culture.

These readers, the doubles of the writers themselves, take pleasure from a reading experience which is not only didactic—Latin American literature will always contain social criticism—but literary. The essays that follow are a homage to those readers. They seek to enhance literary pleasure by associating Spanish American literary texts with works from the Anglo-American tradition. They do not seek to reveal sources but to draw parallels, to show how writers from vastly different corners of the Western tradition manipulate the same devices, how these writers are all shaped by the power of the very genres they attempt to use for their own purposes, how the idea of literary history must be reconsidered—how it must become synchronic or nonlinear in order to deal successfully with its subject. These essays are exploratory in that they reach no hard-and-fast conclusions. Their purpose is to discover points of convergence and divergence as they have occurred to a reader trying to mediate between the antipodes of a civilization that may well, in Spengler's sense, be drifting toward its twilight.

I

Auden, Neruda, and Spain in 1937
Genre and Historical Moment

History is all too often tragic, an unfortunate fact for humanity but a great comfort to historians and authors of historical fictions. The clash of peoples, the rise and fall of nations, conflicts between leaders: These are the dramas that animate both kinds of writing.

While it is usually easy to distinguish history from literature, it is not so easy to keep our roles as readers of history and literature separate. The blurring of these roles—we inevitably take sides in any conflict—produces a crisis for the literary reader because while he accepts, even welcomes, the fact that he must make political or moral evaluations as a reader of history, he finds that such evaluations are irrelevant with regard to literary texts. This lack of relevance carries over, to make matters worse, to those literary works that take history as their subject.

The reader may approach the literary productions of contending parties, both of whom claim to be just and both of whom claim that their cause will ultimately be absolved by history, and find that he either takes no interest in the historical situation behind the texts or that he is incapable of judging that situation in any way. To read a literary text, the reader, insofar as this is possible, must set aside both ideology and history. Which is to say, the historical occasion, the nominal subject of or pretext for the literary work of art, must be forgotten.

This difference between the posture of the author vis-à-vis his subject and the reader vis-à-vis the text is of paramount importance. Unless the reader intends to make literature into history, he must try to remain ideologically neutral. Writers, on the other hand, may do as they please, unless they are working under a specific set of rules—a neoclassical aesthetics or Socialist Realism, for example. Commitment to rules or ideology is, of course, no guarantee of literary success, and the most pious author, the one who believes most firmly in a cause, may bore us.

Some themes are more attractive for literary purposes than others. The celebration of a great victory is an ultimately tedious theme in literature, while suffering and defeat are fascinating: Turnus is more interesting than Aeneas. In the great texts at the center of our culture, the Homeric epics and the Old Testament, victory and defeat are joined in a circular pattern so that neither exists in a pure state. Victors and vanquished, however glorious their acts, are subordinated to fate or the divine will, agencies that do not ordinarily reveal their intentions to mortals. And when they do, in, say, the Bible, the *Aeneid,* or *Paradise Lost,* the goals they set never fully explain the reasons for the struggle, the reasons why the process is necessary. This explanation has been left to teleologically inclined philosophers and literary critics.

When no organic unity, no cyclical conjoining of victory and defeat is available to an author—when he stands, for example, on the losing side—he must attempt to turn defeat into victory by looking towards some struggle that outweighs the lost one at hand. We see this in Lucan, who turns the destruction of the Republic and the defeat of Pompey by Caesar into a moral victory for Cato, in the stoic's triumph over loss of self or integrity in extreme adversity. This moral *Aufhebung*, in which defeat and victory on the physical and political levels are subsumed into an individual's triumph over himself on the personal level, constantly reappears in the Western tradition, from Thermopylae to Masada, from Numantia to the Alamo.

Those who perish for the sake of principle have not died in vain: Their names, because the poet includes them in his poem or the historian in his chronicle, constitute a monument to which humanity may turn for guidance in days of tribulation. The difference between history and literature, and the reason for their inevitable convergence in the reader's mind, is that both are stories. History documents victories and defeats, or merely seeks to record, at the level of chronicle, but as soon as it begins to interpret and attaches greater meaning to events, the events become elements in a plot, pieces of a fiction.

But what about writers who are not able to recall events in tranquility and are obliged to write in the thick of things? Authors, that is, who write *during* wars and project victories that may never come, poets like W. H. Auden and Pablo Neruda who in 1937 compose poems they intend as exhortations to the forces and allies of the Spanish Republic. Today, if we are sympathetic to the fallen Spanish Republic, we read their poems through the idealizing haze of hindsight and nostalgia, inventing meanings for them they may never have had.

To read those poems now, we have to set them into several different contexts: historical, biographical, and literary. To read them as poems on the Spanish Civil War of 1936–39 is at first glance rather an easy task because we see the war as a totality with a coherent shape and a "predictable" outcome, but in 1937 this was not the case. Approaching these poems from the biographical side reduces the civil war to a *psycho-*

machia in which the contending sides become the poet's inner conflicts. A literary reading would locate the poems in a tradition of forms: On the one hand, it renders the historical event the pretext for the poetry, while on the other it treats the poet more as a craftsman seeking to resolve certain technical problems than as an evolving individual. The literary approach to the poems does allow the reader to see them as something more than pious ideological statements and to understand to just how great an extent literary expression is mediated by a finite number of forms, forms that literally rise to the occasion.

Nineteen thirty-seven was a year of ambiguity[1] in the fortunes of the Spanish Republic and a moment of great poetic outpouring by writers sympathetic to the cause of the Republic. Outstanding among the poems produced in that year are Auden's *Spain*,[2] and Pablo Neruda's *España en el corazón: himno a las glorias del pueblo en la querra* (Spain in My Heart: Hymn to the Glories of the People at War)[3]. A comparative reading of these two works reveals that despite ideological affinities they are radically different interpretations of history, interpretations that meant one thing in 1937 and seem to mean something else today.

The first step in this dual literary interpretation is to associate the poems with poetic forms—for *Spain*, the elegy,[4] and for *España en el corazón*, the ode—and to read them as enactments of these divergent but complementary forms.

Setting aside metrical distinctions, the question of whether a given poem is an elegy or an ode depends to a great extent on the *persona* the poet adopts within the composition. Elegies, especially in the sense in which the form is understood here, require a *persona* that is a single voice speaking for itself. Odes on the other hand—and particularly those, like Neruda's, called hymns—constitute a collective statement, whose *per-*

sona is that of a collectivity. It is useful to distinguish between the elegy, the lament of the individual singer, and the ode, the chorus's combined statement, using this difference between individual and group because it helps the reader distinguish between the poetic *persona*'s expression of a private emotion and the poetic *persona* as a voice speaking through and for a community (real or imagined). The difference between *Spain* and *España en el corazón*, the difference between elegy and ode, enables us to trace the development of two very different kinds of twentieth-century poet and to establish a rhetorical (literary) framework for the two texts. To do this we must set aside 1937 and the war and turn to the history of elegies and odes.

Elegy and ode have traditionally been used as vehicles for occasional verse: In ages that appreciate and demand formal statements at significant moments (royal births or deaths, marriages, jubilees), elegies and odes are molds in which poets fit their expressive energies. Naturally these same forms may be turned upside down through irony—the unintentional irony generated by a bad poet or a bad reader—and the celebratory form may actually ridicule a great occasion by rendering its occasional poetry absurd. The intentional irony of the mock or parodic elegy or ode has been the traditional weapon of the political enemies of ruling houses or prime ministers.

In the late twentieth century, our need for stylized verbal statements (serious or parodic) is slight, probably because of the influence of the news media on our perception of history. Scenes of collective suffering make the individual lament insignificant, while, at the same time, our collective emotions are represented as mass emotional outpourings whose image on the television screen makes the need for a poem to express collective emotion superfluous. The thing itself has, in effect, taken the place of the poem.

An even more important reason for the decline of occasional poetry is literary history. Romanticism, despite its rich stock of elegies and odes, transformed all lyric poetry into the chronicle of personal experience, the redaction of a fragmentary autobiography. To talk or sing about another (except through the impersonality of mass media) is to talk or sing about oneself: The commemorative poetical forms have become mirrors for the poet.

The reaction against this "cult of personality," by the Symbolists and many early twentieth-century avant-garde groups, has been strong, but even the anti-Romantic poet must pass through a Romantic phase of self-expression. This abstract *biographia literaria* takes the poet on a journey in which he purges the Romantic poet out of himself. The cure, it seems, is always incomplete, and nostalgia, a longing after the Golden Calf of unbridled self-expression, is a specter that haunts all post-Romantic poets.

The poet who discovers that the ego and its vicissitudes are devoid of intrinsic poetic value may seek consolation and self-justification from something that allows him to transcend his individuality. This might be nature; it might (especially for Existentialist poets) be an ideology or a religion. It might be poetry itself, as in the case of Mallarmé and Wallace Stevens. Rimbaud's high-flown and sardonic pronouncements in his May 15, 1871, letter to Paul Demeny about egoist poets is an early definition of the post-Romantic dilemma:

The first study for a man who wants to be a poet is the knowledge of himself, complete. He looks for his soul, inspects it, puts it to the test, learns it. As soon as he knows it, he must cultivate it! It seems simple: in every brain a natural development takes place; so many *egoists* proclaim themselves authors; there are plenty of others who attribute their intellectual progress to themselves! But the soul has to be made monstrous. . . . I say one must be a *seer*, make oneself a seer.[5]

The process Rimbaud delineates is almost an inversion of psychoanalysis: Instead of rehabilitating the self, Rimbaud seeks to discover the self and let it expand until it reaches its own limits. Ontology writes its own plot, which is episodic, even picaresque, until it illuminates itself in self-contemplation.

To persist in the mode of Rimbaud's *egoists* is to relegate oneself to a single instant of literary history. This is the fate of the avant-garde writer of the early decades of the century. In fact, so much avant-garde verse is self-affirmation, despite protestations to the contrary, that it is difficult to imagine how avant-garde poets did not come to see themselves as parodies of one another. The doctrines of "make it new" and "attack the literary establishment" became so shopworn so quickly it is astonishing there was a bourgeois left to *épater.*

Since they feared they would not be incorporated into the very tradition they professed to despise, avant-garde writers rewrote literary history (or tried to erase it, as Dada did) in order to have it begin or end with them. By the same token, poets who do not transgress, who do not make the *egoist*'s statement of self-affirmation, find themselves in a cul-de-sac. All poets except those who restrict themselves either to an avant-garde or to a received tradition, must pass through a phase of self-affirming destruction (as Harold Bloom describes it in his *Anxiety of Influence*) that is followed by a phase of consolidation: The rebel or outcast poet returns to his reconstituted tradition or his reordered society (if not both) and glorifies it. Or, to use Bartlett Giamatti's terminology, the outlawed Proteus-poet becomes the Orphic extoller of the social order.[6]

Both Auden and Neruda follow this two-phase pattern of development: Their professional trajectories, while leading to quite different results, are, in the abstract, remarkably similar. It is almost as if both had profited from the (perhaps spurious) preface to the *Aeneid* ("Ille ego, qui qondam gracili modulatus avena . . .") or Spenser's echo of it in the first stanza of the *Faerie Queene* ("Lo I the man, whose Muse whilome did maske, / as time her taught, in lowly Shepheards weeds . . ."). These stages, in which the poet deliberately moves on to new forms, moments in the ideal growth of the poet from pastoral to epic, from the light and personal to the grand and social, provide a model against which we measure the development of these two twentieth-century poets.

The differences arise from the relationship of poets like Virgil and Spenser to forms: The eclogue, the sonnet, and the other shorter forms teach the poet his craft; the epic allows him to put all his knowledge and wisdom into practice. It is the supreme text. That is, as readers we are not concerned with the poet's personal development over the years; his sincerity or originality also do not concern us: The poet is simply required to be a virtuoso, one who excels at his craft and is inspired. Only after he has freed himself from the burden of his Romantic ego is the twentieth-century poet able to gain the same sort of control over language as his ancient counterparts. Consistent with this change is his turn (or return) to traditional forms, another sign of his acquiescence to tradition.

Much of the criticism written about twentieth-century poetry remains chained to Romantic aesthetics. The critic has the same problem as the poet: How to judge the poem except by guessing at the author's sincerity when he wrote it? How to determine a poem's worth without relating it to a moral code? How to understand a poem except in terms of the author's life? Stylistic criticism (especially as practiced by Leo

Spitzer, whose essay on Claudel sheds a great deal of light on the modern ode)[7] opened a path to a different understanding of the text, although its methods led occasionally to interpretive errors which biographically oriented critics were only too happy to point out.

These difficulties—poetry as autobiography versus poetry as aesthetic manipulation of language—swarm around the 1937 texts by Auden and Neruda. Critics regard these works as pivotal in the writing of both authors, but deal with them—with some important exceptions-as mere statements of ideology instead of as works of art. It is as though the combined weight of historical occasion and biography were too much for literary criticism to bear, and the result is that *Spain* and *España en el corazón* have ceased to be literary texts and have become statements by the poets in an imaginary interview with history.

The prevailing opinion of Auden's poem among critics who fuse literature, history, and biography may be summarized by a series of statements by Frederick Buell.[8] Buell's reading turns *Spain* into a reflection of Auden's life:

Auden's last major left-wing poem, "Spain 1937," was written about the Spanish Civil War; the poem has an uneasiness that is due in large part to Auden's attempt to blend the youthful iconoclastic extravagance of his literary-political group with the unyielding facts of an imminently tragic political occasion. (p.7)

Read in this way, the poem is Auden's settling of accounts with his own youth; the politics of adolescence give way and Auden evinces a new sense of his relationship to society, one in which his iconoclasm is certainly attenuated. Buell also endows Auden with foreknowledge of the Republic's defeat—which would have made writing the poem superfluous.

As to the poem itself, Buell says:

Instead of evoking the heroism, nobility, and tragic
death of fighters for the Spanish Republic or instead of
trying in some other way to give the events of the war
some particularly "poetic" character or particularly
appalling grotesqueness, Auden's "Spain 1937"
evokes what seems to be the full range and variety of
human life and history, a life and history that accent
their ordinariness by containing more than a fair share
of the trivial and the absurd. The emphasis is upon all
the various human things that happen with the flow
of time and which would be happening in just as
greatly disconnected profusion today if it were not for
Spain's crisis; to capture this sense of profusion, Auden draws on a great wealth of detail and of ideas and
finds a variety of rhetorics in which to embody them,
and contrary to what one would expect, the lists do
not often become flat or chaotic. The brilliance of the
rhetoric and the finesse with which different rhetorical forms are mixed makes most details in the lists
entertaining (and, thus, apparently significant) in and
of themselves. (p.148)

Buell seeks to define the poem through description, by
listing what he sees as its salient characteristics, but
his faint praise for Auden's "rhetoric"—an unfortunately vague term—paves the way for a later damning
of the poem:

"Spain 1937" does not find a voice in which myth and
reality successfully interrelate with one another; even
though Auden may point up his rhetoric as fictional
at the same time he is using it, the poem's chief
source of pleasure lies in the ease with which historical event becomes rhetorical and not in the moral
intensity with which that rhetoric is criticized. Similarly, the voice of "Spain 1937" is one in which the
private pleasure derived from its rhetoric is not recon-
cilable with its public purpose; its verbal elegance sits

only uneasily with the didactic intention, for the former implies a self-gratifying consciousness that,
despite all claims to the contrary, is incompatible
with the vulgar historical world of boring pamphlets
and crude action. (p.156)

Buell knows something is wrong with *Spain*, that its
"rhetoric" conflicts with its didacticism, although
how rhetoric and didacticism can be separated so
sharply is difficult to imagine. The schism Buell sees
enables him to imagine an ideal poem superior to the
one he is reading, as if somewhere there existed the
poem's ideal form. *Spain* fails because it does not live
up to Buell's nonexistent model poem.

Read as an elegy, *Spain* is not the poem Buell describes. First, with regard to its form: While *Spain* is
written in blank verse, it is arranged in quatrains, the
traditional elegiac stanza in English. Auden's quatrains
have a Latinate cadence, derived, in the first six
strophes, from the repetition of the dactyl "yesterday."
While the meter of Auden's verses conforms to no specific elegiac model, the strophes—unrhymed and therefore "impure"—allude to a form; they are enough of an
allusion to evoke both the elegiac tradition as a tradition of form and that same tradition in terms of its
subject matter. It is as though Auden were content to
evoke a (perhaps Horatian) tradition even if he were
unwilling to abide absolutely by its rules. This would
also be consistent with the post-Romantic poet's coming to grips with both his individuality and the traditional tools of his profession.

The first six quatrains juxtapose "yesterday" with
"today." "Yesterday" includes not only the poet's personal past but "all the past," the international market
economy, "the invention / Of cartwheels and clocks,"
the progressive loss of myth ("the abolition of fairies
and giants"), and the growth of science. As Edward
Mendelson puts it:

The poem presents a cataclysmic account of human time, organized according to Auden's characteristic pattern of two integrated periods separated from each other by a third, divided one. "Yesterday all the past," the poem begins, initiating six stanzas of grand synechdochal panorama that embrace all of time from the aboriginal taming of horses to the romantic adoration of madmen. "To-morrow, perhaps the future," it tentatively predicts in four of its later stanzas, looking toward a time of "perfect communion" and "the rediscovery of romantic love." Between these two periods is "to-day the struggle."[9]

Mendelson is absolutely correct in pointing out that "In *Spain* Auden makes his first real effort to describe the transition from division to unity, from the struggling present to the fulfilled future" (*Early Auden*, pp.316–17) but, curiously enough, the antithesis of yesterday in the poem is not tomorrow but today, and it is in this opposition that Auden presents his first paradox.

Yesterday was ignorance, yesterday was technological accomplishment, but all yesterdays are meaningless in the face of the dilemma of today: "the struggle." Just what "the struggle" is is not entirely clear despite the fact that Spain in 1937 is the obvious subject of the poem. This is the case because Spain is not the only subject. The poem also deals with the narrator himself. That is, the struggle involves the *persona* adopted by the poet which enables him to participate in the action instead of chronicling and interpreting what has already happened. It is as though the definition of today as "the struggle," with all the dramatic connotations the word has, gives the narrator his first chance to be an actor, to change the circumstances he evokes.

Mendelson sees the poem in a different way, one that reflects Auden's self-contradicting view of individual action and morality in the context of a predetermined notion of history. Mendelson points out that Auden's partiality for the Republic obliges him to link the fate of the Republic to the utopian flow of history while it forces him to link the fascist forces to those energies seeking to hold back the inevitable march of history. Republican violence, therefore, is good, while General Franco's violence is evil. Mendelson analyzes this conclusion:

Yet the war as a whole is a projection of our inner struggle between hatred and love, a struggle that occurs in everyone. The poem maintains simultaneously that the war projects "our" division and that those of us who fight on the correct side are undivided. Auden manages to have it both ways by suggesting that those who fight on the correct side are exempt from the human condition, that for them the undivided future has already arrived as the charity of warriors. So while the poem's manifest argument asserts that all human actions are chosen by the will, the metaphoric argument maintains that some special actions in the political realm, actions directed at certain social goals, are the product not of will but of something very much like unconscious instinctive nature. (*Early Auden*, p. 319)

There is no way to apologize for this self-contradiction in *Spain*; at the same time, we must remember that Auden is writing a poem of exhortation, that he must create what Northrop Frye calls "participation mystique" (*Anatomy*, p.295) if his poem is to have any effect on the community he is addressing. It is in this that Auden's elegy drifts toward the ode, drifts, that is, from the personal expression of emotion to a collective expression. But the transition is incomplete because the poem remains personal and elegiac rather than communal or ode-like.

After the first six quatrains, the narrator summons all like-minded people to participate in the struggle, and this invitation to others to reconstitute themselves, to transform themselves from observers into actors, is the subject of the next eight stanzas. First the narrator presents us with two figures who seek external guidance: the poet, who appeals to inspiration ("O my vision. O send me the luck of the sailor.") and "the investigator," who "peers through his instruments" at the microscopic (the "virile bacillus") or at the colossal ("enormous Jupiter"), but who must "inquire," must ask someone else about the "lives of my friends." Instead of looking within for the moral solutions to the struggle they confront, these characters shirk responsibility and look to external sources. In doing so, they lose their chance to attain an identity. The self created by the self may well be a fiction, but it has at least the virtue of being one's own handiwork, the result of a decision made on one's own.

The next two characters are the poor and the nation-states. The poor are the disinherited, those who live even today without the consolations of technology. They are cold, hopeless, and begging for consolation: "Our day is our loss, O show us / History the operator, the / Organiser, Time the refreshing river." They want the promise of a utopia they can never enjoy, a story or plot that will give meaning and solace to their meaningless lives. The nation-states, egoistic individuals with the desires and fears of individuals, ask for intervention by the life force: "Did you not found the city state of the sponge, // Raise the vast military empires of the shark / And the tiger, establish the robin's plucky canton? / Intervene. O descend as a dove or / A furious papa or a mild engineer, but descend."

Justin Replogle astutely comments on this satiric passage of comic denunciation: "When men fervently yearn for some change, they will turn everywhere but to themselves for a cure. Some god out of the machine, they hope will turn up fortuitously to secure them:

Christ, or a Freudian father figure, or an eighteenth century deist God."[10] Life, in the poem the energy that animates all creatures which is personified by those seeking external justification or guidance, denies its transcendental status, affirms its immanence, its being part of the questioner, and throws the problem back to the nation-states. As it does so, it declares its shadow or echo-like status: "I am whatever you do." It concludes with a definition and a challenge: "I am your choice, your decision. Yes, I am Spain."

At this point the existential crux becomes an elegy. The choice has been made, if not consciously then tacitly: The nation- states choose to do nothing on behalf of Spain. This decision provokes a reaction among individuals, the subject of the next five stanzas. Many rush to the defense of the Spanish Republic: "Many have heard it on remote peninsulas, / On sleepy plains, in the aberrant fisherman's islands/ Or the corrupt heart of the city, / Have heard and migrated like gulls or the seeds of a flower." Those who come may die, but they will die as individuals who have achieved this status by making a deliberate and—for Auden—correct choice. Their decision to fight for the Republic has its poetic antecedent in Lucan's *Pharsalia*, where Cato decides to fight along with Pompey (whom he despises) against Caesar. It is a decision to maintain his moral integrity which obliges the individual to confront the imminent danger of death, yet one more challenge to his moral integrity.

The final seven stanzas of *Spain* complete the dialectical process begun at the outset: the "yesterday" of the beginning and the "to-day" of the struggle are subsumed into the "To-morrow, perhaps the future." To-morrow, should it come and should the *persona* be alive to witness it, will bring a return to routines: professions, experiments, even "romantic love." But the synthesis will remain incomplete until the historical process set into motion by the decision or indecision of millions of individuals runs its course. To commit oneself to the struggle of today means hurling oneself into the world of contingency and expediency—a commitment Auden explicitly repudiates in the 1965 preface to his *Collected Poems*. Morality in *Spain* is determined by the occasion: "To-day the deliberate increase in the chance of death, / The conscious acceptance of guilt in the necessary murder; / To-day the expending of powers / On the flat pamphlet and the boring meeting." There is no escape from the wheel of fortune, but the individual may console himself for his own death and that of others by declaring that he has acted because he has taken on the responsibility for all of mankind, a kind of ominous revision of the Kantian categorical imperative. Of course, only history can determine whether or not it is the "correct" decision.

The final strophe again presents the privileged individual who is able to stand for an instant on the bank of history and consider his next action. The river flows on inexorably, the time for deciding is short, and the tools for arriving at a decision inadequate. He will, however, decide: "The stars are dead. The animals will not look. / We are left alone with our day, and the time is short, and / History to the defeated / May say Alas but cannot help nor pardon." The narrator pays ironic homage to the elegist's traditional use of the pathetic fallacy: Nature here will not weep at what happens in human affairs because it is a vast machine. And in this it is like history, the cold redaction of past events.

Our historical perspective on the Spanish Civil War makes us see irony in Auden's use of the elegy. His cause was—though not in the moment he wrote the poem—a lost one, and his poem seems now to be a defiant praise of those who made the "correct" decision despite the hopelessness of the situation, a hopelessness Auden could not have seen as he wrote. *Spain*

enters easily into the catalogue of poems on defeat, elegies written to honor the fallen in battle. And the interpretation is not erroneous because Auden's use of
the elegy invites just such an interpretation. His choice
may derive, as Mendelson says, from internal conflicts:

In the late 1930s, on the battlefields of Auden's
poems, two literary traditions, two ideologies of art,
struggle for supremacy. He was trying to escape the
modernist poetic he had renounced earlier but to
which he found himself returning as he wrote poems
in opposition to his beliefs. He had set out to write in
a tradition that engaged the problems of choice and
action, and performed a didactic function in the society around it. But when he actually wrote his political
poems he used the formal and rhetorical methods of a
tradition that claimed to be independent of existing
society, superior to its vulgar concerns. What made
the struggle between these two traditions so difficult
to resolve was that the forces of one side had successfully disguised themselves in the uniform of the
other. (*Early Auden*, p.202)

After the nineteen thirties[11] and after World War II,
Auden reconciles his personal poetic voice with the literary heritage he realized was his own. The elegy on
Spain marks a moment of transition in this growth: It
blends exhortation—the poet addressing an audience—with a private meditation on the structures of
history. It expresses the hope that the wheel of fortune
will turn in a favorable way and that the "struggle"
will resolve itself in victory—although even this hope
is rendered ambiguous by the last verse: "History to
the defeated / May say Alas but cannot help nor pardon." If we read the poem out of its historical context,
we may find in it a baroque "desengaño," the realization that to expect one's personal morality to be the
morality of nation-states is the worst sort of pathetic
fallacy, that the individual can only decide things

(when fortune grants him that rare privilege) for himself. *Spain* transcends both the occasion and the poet: It is the triumph of a form, a demonstration of how the poet can address history and express himself yet have his creation stolen away by the literary tradition.

Before 1937, Auden and Neruda represented two specific kinds of poet, Auden the poet of wit, Neruda the poet of passion. Neruda blends the legacy of the Spanish Baroque (filtered through Romanticism and Spanish American *Modernismo*—itself a synthesis of Romanticsm and Symbolism) with the fragmented, hallucinatory poetry typical of the avant-garde of the first two decades of this century. Auden combines elements of eighteenth-century didacticism with Romanticism and Symbolism. This earlier phase of development inclines each poet toward a specific form when the moment comes to write a political poem: Neruda turns to the ode (which he calls a hymn) and Auden to the elegy. After 1937, Auden's poetic *persona* is usually personal and individual, while Neruda consciously takes on a collective persona, striking the pose of the inspired prophet,[12] who reveals not the future but the truth of the present, who is both a satirist and the voice of the oppressed peoples of the Americas, Walt Whitman as Communist ideologue.

The visionary, the satirist, and the prophet come together in *España en el corazón,* subtitled *Himno a las glorias del pueblo en la guerra.* Neruda's use of the word "hymn" here points out just what he hopes to accompish and, paradoxically, just what his poem cannot achieve. It is impossible to separate the hymn from divine worship, from a community's relationship to God. Thus, in elevating the "people" to the condition of deity, Neruda evokes in this title the hymn's "radical of presentation" in order to conjure up Frye's "participation mystique." The poet's "I" becomes a communal "I," just as the generic designation "hymn" constitutes an attempt to overcome or transcend individuality. The poet-prophet is one with his people: They speak through him; he is their voice. But because there is no divinity present in the poem except at the level of rhetoric, we must assume Neruda is really writing an ode and not a hymn, that Neruda's voice remains his own. Paul Fry has elucidated the peculiar relationship between hymn and ode:

Only the hymn speaks from knowledge, while the ode always hopes for knowledge. . . . Perhaps there is no such thing as a hymn of participation; if so, then the difference between hymn and ode is simply the difference between common prayer and personal prayer. By imitating hymnody, however, an ode reveals *its* conception of a hymn as a being-present to a transcendent, originary voice. The aim of the ode is to recover and usurp the voice to which hymns defer: not merely to participate in the presence of voice but to *be* the voice.[13]

Fry's remarks apropos of Shelly's "Hymn to Intellectual Beauty" enable us to see just what is at stake in Neruda's "hymn": "In the opening lines [Shelley] pretends that his incomparably esoteric numen is an object of common prayer by singing apparently in behalf of a congregation. . . . Hereafter the poem lapses into the first-person singular and the language of private experience, by no means with the purpose of declaring, with collective intimacy, "A mighty fortress is my God." Shelley's hymn is an ode" (*Poet's Calling*, p.8). We may assume, with Fry, irony on Shelley's part and, in Neruda's case, a sincere desire for community. The result for both poets is, nevertheless, an ode.

Neruda invokes the hymn modality in order to sing a song of praise to the Spanish people and to encourage them in a time of trouble. But there is much more than exhortation in *España en el corazón*, precisely because it is not a hymn. It contains a fragment of autobiography (as do Claudel's odes), a great deal of invective against the Nationalists, commemorations of battles, a lyrical evocation of Madrid in 1937, an encomium of the International Brigade, and a final, prophetic paean to the People's Army. Auden's elegy deals with the individual's need to make decisions in order to maintain his identity and integrity:a stoic, Lucanesque attitude toward death. Neruda's ode exhorts those on the "good" side to fight on, to victory or death. As Fry says, "The ode differs from elegy . . . chiefly in coming upon death while meaning to talk about birth; whereas in the typical movement of an elegy it is the other way around" (*Poet's Calling*, p.13). Auden's melancholy voice preaches a lesson about living, while Neruda's impassioned hymn directs its audience into the jaws of death.

It is absolutely essential we keep in mind the ideas of persona and "radical of presentation": The poet Neruda is not Neruda the man,[14] just as Walt the titanic singer of America is not Walt Whitman, and *España en el corazón* only makes sense if we understand that the poet aspires to speak for a collectivity. His autobiographical interpolation both destroys his prophetic role in an absolute sense and, paradoxically, affirms it. This brief lapse into individuality would have been appropriate in a measured, elegiac self-analysis in Auden's style, a way of documenting how a conversion took place, but Neruda, through his persona, tells instead why a poet of self-expression, of anguished and gigantic ego—one who even here uses his most idiosyncratic metaphors—had to abandon himself and become a socially committed, post-Romantic poet.

The "old man" (in the religious sense) is not dead, just swept aside by circumstance. Neruda, then, is fusing two rhetorics he had previously kept separate, the rhetoric of poetry and the rhetoric of ideology. The occasion of the Civil War is, to be sure, the crucible in which they fuse, but the process had begun earlier, specifically in Neruda's translation of William Blake's *Visions of the Daughters of Albion* and "The Mental Traveller," which he published in the Spanish magazine *Cruz y raya* in 1934.[15]

Neruda's criteria in selecting Blake texts for a Spanish audience are entirely personal. "The Mental Traveller" and *The Visions of the Daughters of Albion* document moments in the cyclical, recurring failure of mankind to achieve what in Blake's terms "Humanity Divine Incomprehensible" attains at the end of *Jerusalem* IV. In that text the Four Faces of Humanity converse:

> And they conversed together in Visionary forms
>   dramatic which bright
> Redounded from their Tongues in thunderous
>   majesty, in Visions
> In new Expanses, creating exemplars of Memory
>   and of Intellect,
> Creating Space, creating Time, according to the
>   wonders Divine
> Of Human Imagination throughout all the Three
>   Regions immense
> Of Childhood, Manhood & Old Age.[16]

This is the moment when the Imagination reaches autonomy, the "Spectre" of doubt banished, when the poet is not "pure and disposed to rise to the stars," but capable of creating the cosmos through his own visionary powers. "To me this world is all one continued vision of Fancy or Imagination . . . " says Blake in a letter to Reverend Trusler, a statement that makes him equal to Rimbaud in postulating a visionary self that would transcend egoism.

"The Mental Traveller" describes the abject human condition: sexual differentiation, instinctive breeding, inability to rise above contingency. The narrator of the poem is a superhuman observer who describes the newborn child as the fruit of contradiction ("born in joy / begotten in dire woe"), and how, if he is male, he is given to an old woman who "nails him down upon a rock, / catches his shrieks in cups of gold." As the boy matures, the woman grows younger: He turns into an aged wanderer, she into a maiden. He pursues her madly until he becomes, once again, an infant. At the end, he is "the frowning Babe," in a grotesque nativity scene. Harold Bloom comments:

Where the first half of the poem described the mutual betrayals between man and nature, the second is concerned with man's failure to transmute nature into art, but again the guilt is double. The Poor Man, as he has become, finds a Maiden again, in an earlier phase than that of the one who rejected him for an earlier vision of himself. But he has learned nothing from his defeats, and this embrace costs him the remnants of his imaginative vision.[17]

The only way this ever-worsening process of repetition can be stopped is through an explosion of the imagination.

The Visions of the Daughters of Albion also deals with the individual's failure to embrace his own imagination and, like "The Mental Traveller," also concentrates on human sexuality. Here the protagonist is female, Oothoon, raped by Bromion, a lustful thunder deity, as she is on her way to her intended mate Theotormon, an anguished ocean god. Bromion, like Amnon in the story of Absalom, rejects Oothoon as a harlot, but when she turns to Theotormon for consolation she finds only tormented indecision: He can neither love nor despise her. Oothoon is sexually alive in a world where sexuality is repressed. The end of the poem, a kind of *Huit Clos,* describes Oothoon lamenting while "Theotormon sits/ Upon the margin'd ocean conversing with shadows dire" (p.215). The Daughters of Albion, the female chorus of the text, redouble

Oothoon's lamentations, thereby showing that all women share her doom.

The erotic element in Neruda's poetry (1934 is the year of his highly erotic "Las furias y las penas" [furies and sufferings]) finds an echo in the defense of sexuality in the *Visions*, just as Blake's criticism of a society based on repression and the blind acceptance of dogma would also have appealed to him. But even more important to him is the central theme of both "The Mental Traveller" and the *Visions*: the need to transcend social restraints (including orthodox religion) and individuality in order to become visionary. To be a Visionary is to see all (the motto of the *Visions* is "The Eye sees more than the Heart knows") and not to need the comforting rules of society to survive. We cannot know if Neruda ever thought himself a visionary, but we can imagine that in trying to be one he would take on, most poignantly in 1937, the role of *vox populi*, the prophetic voice of the people. Neruda's denunciation of things as they are parallels Blake's, and both evoke a world that might be. In 1937, however, Neruda concentrates on denouncing what is happening during the Spanish Republic's hour of need.

España en el corazón divides into twenty-four parts, the divisions indicated by a word or phrase in the margin, similar to the marginal tags in "The Rime of the Ancient Mariner." Probably copied from biblical annotation, this technique reappears in Neruda's *Canto general*, but he does not use it in his books of lyric poetry, either before or after *España en el corazón,*, no doubt because the *persona* of all those books is a single individual.

The first division of the poem is entitled "Invocación," but who or what the poet seeks to invoke is ambiguous. In the ode, the poet does not follow the model of the epic poet's invocation of the muse to sing through him, in effect to be his memory, although Neruda does to some extent assume the posture of the epic poet here the better to remind the reader of the "arms and the people" aspect of his poem. Nor is Neruda's invocation precisely like the hymn-writer's calling upon God because God, after all, is already present.

His invocation is really an apostrophe. In that device the poet speaks to a place, a person (usually absent), or a *genius loci*, and those mute agencies speak through the poet or allow the poet to blend with them. If we examine Neruda's first poetic sentence, we see it lacks a predicate verb: The two verbs present are an infinitive and part of a modifying clause. This is an extreme example of ellipsis—something important is missing. We see a will or a desire, "la voluntad de un canto / con explosiones, el deseo / de un canto inmenso" ("the desire for a song / with explosions, the desire / for an immense song"), but the "I" who wills or desires carefully excludes reference to himself. The "radical of presentation" is one in which no mention of the singer is necessary, in which the singer is before us, in profound communication with us. He invokes the energy of imagination—inevitably and fatally his own imagination—to provide him with a song, a verbal metaphor for a substance: "un metal que recoja / guerra y desnuda sangre" ("a metal that includes / war and naked blood"). This metal would be a kind of war trumpet, but its blast would include love ("la rosa pura y partida" ["the pure and split rose"]) and cosmology ("el origen / de cielo y aire y tierra" ["the origin / of sky and air and earth"]). In the images of the rose and the song about origins, we see two traditions: the amatory (sacred and profane, the rose is "split") and the prophetic. The poet seeks to convoke the traditional powers of the poet in order to reveal the meaning of what is happening in Spain. To do this he uses the traditional poetic devices, images, and the full panoply of tropes.

Thus invocation becomes apostrophe: The absent power invoked has always been present in the poet; he will make it visible through his text.

The next division is a genuine apostrophe. Neruda addresses his subject: Spain, the motherland ("Madre natal"). His address is a simple question: "¿Quién? por caminos, quién,/ quién, quién? en sombra, en sangre, quién? / en destello, quién,/ quién?" ("Who?, along roads, who, / who, who? in shadow, in blood, who? / in distillation, who / who?"). The poet asks Spain to identify her enemies, those who have turned her into "machacada piedra, combatida ternura, de trigo, cuero y animal ardiendo" ("smashed stone, fought tenderness, of wheat, hide and burning animal"). Neruda calls civil war matricide, a horror suggested in the confrontation between Julius Caesar and the personification of Rome in the *Pharsalia.* The difference is that, in Lucan, Rome speaks while here Neruda speaks for Spain. Suddenly the questioning is interrupted by violent action, the division entitled "Bombardeo" ("Bombardment").

Neruda's rhetorical intention in this section is to approximate the reality of war insofar as words can represent that turmoil. He combines asyndeton and polysyndeton: "Cae / ceniza, cae / hierro / y piedra y muerte y llanto y llamas" ("Falls / ash, falls / iron/ and stone and death and wailing and flames"), a mixture of concrete substances and abstractions that reaffirms the apocalyptic tone set at the beginning in the invocation-apostrophe. Lists are one of Neruda's favorite devices, especially in *Residencia en la tierra* (*Residence on Earth*), and their appearance here indicates that even when Neruda becomes a prophetic poet he does not abandon his earlier hermetic style. He simply subordinates that style to a new intention: Here the topsy--turvy world does not reflect an anguished ego but a situation in which the forces of repression are metaphors for a demonic anti-order. They recreate on an ideological or moral plane the unnamed sources of anguish in Neruda's earlier expressionistic poetry.

The third phase of *España en el corazón,* "Maldición" ("Curse"), is a ritual cursing of the enemy which evokes the magic of satiric vituperation. Ironically, it links Neruda with a poet fighting on the fascist side in the Spanish Civil War, Roy Campbell. In *Flowering Rifle* (1939),[18] which Robert C. Elliott analyzes in *The Power of Satire*[19] as a model of magical invective, Campbell compares his verses to a lasso for catching enemies: "If only once I'd whirled the whistling line/ To get them hog-tied with iambic twine" (*Rifle,* p.23). Neruda's curses, especially in his attacks on Generals Sanjurjo, Mola, and Franco, are, like his attempts to recreate war in language, linguistic raids on reality: Here he wants weave a spell around the enemy generals. This shamanistic desire to use poetry as magic reappears in Neruda's promise that Spain will rise from her own ashes: "Patria surcada, / juro que en tus cenizas / nacerás como flor de agua perpetua, / juro que de tu boca de sed saldrán al aire / los pétalos del pan, la derramada / espiga inaugurada." ("Furrowed father land, / I swear that in your ashes / you will be born like a flower of perpetual water, '/ I swear that from your mouth of thirst will issue into air / the petals of bread, the poured out / inaugurated seed"). There is no inconsistency here because Neruda's interpretation of the ode allows him to mix anything with a call to arms.

The reader is not, therefore, surprised to find an autobiographical section in the text in which Neruda talks about his poetic conversion. "Explico algunas cosas" ("I shall explain a few things") is comparable to those passages in Virgil or Spenser where the poet notes his passage from pastoral to epic poetry. Neruda goes further, virtually parodying the style of his own earlier books, especially *Residencia en la tierra:*

Preguntaréis: ¿Y dónde están las lilas?
Y la metafísica cubierta de amapolas?
Y la lluvia que a menudo golpeaba
Sus palabras llenándolas
De agujeros y pájaros?
Os voy a contar todo lo que me pasa.
(You might ask: Where are the lilies?
And the poppy-covered metaphysics?
And the rain that often beat
On his words filling them
With holes and birds?
I'm going to tell you everything that's going on
   with me.)

Neruda is deliberately conversational and prosaic here in order to point out the sharp division between the present and the past—a past of personal experience and poetic past with its own system of images. He goes on to describe his life in prewar Madrid, his friends Federico García Lorca and Rafael Alberti, the pastoral quality of his flower-covered house and neighborhood despite their urban setting. Then he chronicles the disasters of war, the fire that consumes the idealized past. All that remains is his voice, damning the enemy and urging the reader to come and see the blood flowing in the streets—another device to incorporate the reader into the action.

Neruda dedicates the rest of the poem to listing catastrophes and Republican heroism. Despite his attempts to maintain the hope that a new day will dawn for Spain, his poem becomes increasingly melancholy, almost elegiac. The genre clearly begins to work its effect on the poet at this point. The poet aspires to be the voice of the people, longs to embody its collective spirit, desires both to incite action and to be action, but the very weight of its own rhetorical baggage pulls it back to earth. In the section entitled "Canto sobre unas ruinas" (Song on some ruins), Neruda turns to the

Spanish Baroque for poetic guidance, particularly, as Alain Sicard[20] and others have pointed out, to Rodrigo Caro's "Canción a las ruinas de Itálica" (Song to the ruins of Italica). Neruda begins this section in the demonstrative style of all poems on ruins:

> Esto que fue creado y dominado,
> esto que fue humedecido, usado, visto
> yace—pobre pañuelo—entre las olas
> de tierra y negro azufre.
> (This that was created and dominated,
> this that was moistened, used, seen
> lies—poor handkerchief—among the waves
> of earth and black sulphur.)

Neruda talks about Spain as a geographical and moral reality. much in the way Auden describes the entire Iberian peninsula in *Spain* as a "fragment nipped" from Afica. However, where Auden makes the peninsula into a no-man's-land of existential decision, Neruda links it to the tradition of poems that meditate on ruins as metaphors for the ephemeral nature of life. Rodrigo Caro's "canción" begins:

> Estos, Fabio, ay dolor, que ves ahora
> campos de soledad, mustio collado,
> fueron un tiempo Itálica famosa. . .
> (These, Fabius, oh grief, you see now,
> fields of solitude, parched hill,
> were once famous Italica. . . .)

The two passages complement each other to such an extent that the reader is left wondering whether Neruda is using Rodrigo Caro as a touchstone or as a subject of parody. Is he evoking the great Hispanic tradition of *desengaño,* with its metaphysical invitation to the reader to think about his own "ruin" and his ultimate destiny, or is he mocking that tradition by urging the reader to save Spain from destruction? Despite the oratory of exhortation, the mood here is that of despair.

The rest of *España en el corazón* is an attempt to snatch hope from the ashes of this despair. The final division of the poem, "Oda solar al Ejército del Pueblo" (Solar ode to the People's Army), aside from explicitly linking the entire text to the ode tradition, is an exhortation to the Republican army. But even as he pushes that army forward in space ("adelante, España, / adelante, campanas populares, / adelante, regiones de manzana, / adelante, estandartes cereales, mayúsculos del fuego" [forward, Spain, / forward, bells of the people, / forward, apple regions, / forward, cereal standards, capital letters of fire]) in a desire to push it forward in time, to the time of victory, the poem seems to confess its inherent despair.

Neruda tells the army that all the implements the people use would like to march with them ("cada instrumento, cada rueda roja, / cada mango de sierra o penacho de arado, / cada extracción del suelo, cada temblor de sangre / quiere seguir tus pasos, Ejército del Pueblo" [every instrument, every red wheel, / every saw handle, every plow handle, / everything taken from the soil, every pulse of blood / wants to follow your steps, People's Army]) to that ever-more abstract victory. In conclusion, he tells the army:

> tu luz organizada llega a los pobres hombres
> olvidados, tu definida estrella
> clava sus roncos rayos en la muerte
> y establece los nuevos ojos de la esperanza.
> (your organized light reaches poor, forgotten
> men, your defined star
> sinks its hoarse points in death
> and fixes the new eyes of hope.)

Neruda's ode ends with the word "hope," certainly a tentative notion for a poem that sets out to move an army and a people on to victory. Surely what we see is the ode itself collapsing under the burden of its own tropes, of the individual poet reappearing as the collective voice he sought to embody dissolves, leaving him, as before, alone.

Auden's *Spain* and Neruda' *España en el corazón* are two kinds of poetic response to the Spanish situation in 1937. Auden seeks to transform the variously private and didactic poetry of his earlier career into the formal elegy in order to delineate that moment in which an abstract individual—the reader—may arrive at a "correct" decision about morality and history. Neruda, the poet of anguished self-expression, turns to the ode to try to take on the collective persona of the prophet. Auden's meditation is measured, controlled by the exigencies of his form, while Neruda's form allows him to curse, praise, and exhort within a single framework. Both poems demonstrate how in a moment when one might expect a poet to speak directly "from the heart" just the opposite occurs, how the moment the reader expects an absolutely personal performance in the Romantic manner, he gets just the opposite.

The plot of history is tortuous, and the history of literature is a labyrinth. Auden and Neruda write poems to support the Spanish Republic, poems that call upon the reader to fight or to cheer the People's Army on to victory. But the very moment the two write they find themselves constrained by genre, parodied by the very genres they hope to use, and it is suddenly the genre that speaks instead of the poet.

To the reader who comes after the fact the form may be the first step in misinterpretation: Should he take Auden's elegy at its word and read it as a lamentation? Should he read Neruda's ode as a self-defeating celebration of a never-to-come victory or simply as a premature poem in honor of the fallen defeated, a poem in the mode of Allen Tate's "Ode to the Confederate Dead"? The strange work of time and interpretation renders these texts ambiguous and reminds us that meaning, despite authorial intention and generic deter-mination, rests with the ever-changing understanding of the reader.

2

Countries of the Mind:
Literary Space in Joseph Conrad
and José Donoso

Borges begins his 1938 review of *Absalom, Absalom!* by comparing Faulkner to Joseph Conrad:

I know of two kinds of writer: one whose obsession is verbal procedure, and one whose obsession is the work and passions of men. The former tends to receive the derogatory label "Byzantine" and to be exalted as a "pure artist." The other, more fortunate, has known such laudatory epithets as "profound," "human," "profoundly human," and the flattering abuse of "primal." . . . Among the great novelists, Joseph Conrad was the last, perhaps, who was as interested in the procedures of the novel as in the destiny and personality of his characters. The last, until Faulkner's sensational appearance on the scene.[1]

Borges's association of Conrad with Faulkner reflects the powers of his imagination: In reviewing Faulkner, he looks beyond the southern, regional writer and discovers an artist concerned with both character and the problems of narrative structure. That is, he reminds us that Faulkner is as concerned with technique as he is with his obsessive themes. He then casts about for a parallel and finds Conrad: The mere act tells the critic a great deal about levels of reader response. On the one hand, Borges acknowledges that in the works of both there is the immediate appeal of theme and character, but he points out at the same time that there is another, perhaps more occult dimension to their writing, their modification of their immediate narrative tradition.

Borges has always had an antipathy toward the novel, preferring, when he condescends to speak favorably about extended fictions, what he calls, in his 1940 prologue to Adolfo Bioy Casares's novella *The Invention of Morel*, "the novel of adventures,"[2] fictions that have (according to him) a rigorously organized cause-and-effect plot. His sibylline remarks prod us into speculation: What are the "procedures of the novel" Borges contrasts in that prologue with the "destiny and personality" of the characters? Except for his insistence in his 1932 essay "Narrative Art and Magic"[3] on the need for unity of plot, Borges goes no further with his "morphology of the novel":

To my knowledge, no one has yet attempted a history of the forms of the novel, a morphology of the novel. Such a hypothetical and just history would emphasize the name of Wilkie Collins, who inaugurated the curious method of entrusting the narration of a work to the characters; of Robert Browning, whose vast narrative poem, *The Ring and the Book* (1868), details the same crime ten times, through ten months and ten souls; of Joseph Conrad, who at times showed two interlocutors guessing and reconstructing the story of a third. Also—with obvious justice—of William Faulkner.[4]

This is a curious list and a curious aesthetics of the novel, one vaguely based on the idea of the literary text's tendency, as the Russian Formalists would have it, to call attention to its mechanisms, in effect to make the display of its mechanisms a part of its very structure. Collins's *The Moonstone*, Browning's *The Ring and the Book*, and Conrad's *The Secret Agent*—if this is the novel by Conrad to which Borges alludes—

are all eccentric works that constitute a parodic commentary on novelistic Realism.

What interests Borges is an author's subtle revolt against tradition and his almost imperceptible challenge to his readers to take note of his experiment. This is why Borges does not include Joyce or Virginia Woolf in the list: Their innovations are blatant attempts to modify both the narrative tradition and the reader's relationship to the text. Borges certainly admires these daring innovators, as his essays on Joyce and Woolf demonstrate, but his personal affinities lie with the kind of writer he includes in the list above, those whose experiments are veiled by an outward adherence to convention.

After 1932, the mature Borges is much more interested in the ironic parody of literary conventions rather than in an avant-garde assault on any literary establishment, as his own fictions prove. What makes Borges a fascinating if idiosyncratic critic is his ability to find aspects of the writers he likes that few critics ever see, for example, the idea that Joseph Conrad is as important a writer in his parodic manipulations of narrative structure as he is in the creation of intense psychological portraits. Borges's assertions about Conrad make us see Conrad in a different light and make us question our received notions about him. This is especially true of *Nostromo* (1904),[5] usually read as a political novel. Eloise Knapp Hay defines *Nostromo* in this way:

Nostromo is primarily a novel of ideas, and its theme (seen especially in the contrast between the materialisms of the idealist Gould and the simple Nostromo) evolves as a revelation of the logic of ideas in history. With the demise of Martin Decoud, and the ascent of Dr. Monygham in the last part of the novel, however, we mark a rejection—characteristic of Conrad—of ideas, of intellectuality, and an invocation of moral sensibility . . . as the proper guide for political action.[6]

Hay dissects *Nostromo* in order to find the organization of its intellectual structure, but she loses patience with the novel as an aesthetic structure:

In short, I find that this disorderly presentation (in Part I) of material contributes greatly to the novel's "dramatic impenetrability" (as Morton Dauwen Zabel calls it) and its "hollow" reverberation (F. R. Leavis). It has not the chronological suggestiveness of *Lord Jim*, where the reader need not wonder distractedly for two hundred pages whether his human interest—the only worthy interest in a novel—is to be given anywhere a worthy object. (p.176)

Hay does not explain what she means by "human interest, " but it no doubt has something to do with Borges's second type of writer, the one "whose obsession is the work and passions of men." Hay's dissatisfaction with the first part of *Nostromo* typifies the attitude of most Conrad critics since F. R. Leavis. Hay's reaction and her comparision of *Nostromo*'s "disorderly presentation of materials" with *Lord Jim*'s "chronological suggestiveness" reflect an all-too-common trend in Anglo-American literary criticism: What is unclear or ambiguous is not good. Even if, as Leavis says, *Nostromo* is "one of the great novels of the language,"[7] it is flawed.

There is something unsettling in this mixture of literary criticism and aesthetic evaluation: The critic wants to show the patterns of Conrad's political novels, but she also wants to tell us that *Nostromo* does not meet some unspecified standard. Conrad critics, from Leavis to Hay, have subordinated Conrad's "verbal procedures" to his themes. In doing so they have reawakened the ancient (and false) opposition of form to content; they have, in short, not read Conrad as a novelist but as an essayist. He is "good" when he presents his subjects in an orderly way and he is "bad" when he does not. A reading of *Nostromo* that would take Conrad's "verbal procedures" into account and think of them as consubstantial with his themes is possible.

We see this already in Leavis's essay on Conrad, where he states:

What doesn't seem to be a commonplace is the way in which the whole book forms a rich and subtle but highly organized pattern. Every detail, character and incident has its significant bearing on the themes and motives of this. The magnificence referred to above addresses the senses, or the sensuous imagination; the pattern is one of moral significance. (p.232)

Leavis gestures toward the structure of *Nostromo*, but immediately returns to his primary concern, theme. *Nostromo*'s plot does, however, clarify the relationship between theme and structure and shows just how subtle an innovator Conrad is.

Eloise Knapp Hay's remark about *Lord Jim*'s "chronological suggestiveness"—which *Nostromo* certainly lacks—is an unwitting insight. It is precisely Conrad's eccentricity, his being an *outsider*, an interloper in the Western tradition and not a native-born English novelist that we see in the structure of *Nostromo*. He eschews chronology and the progressive view of history that informs the nineteenth-century European novel, and this links him to the parodic literature of twentieth-century Latin America. His attitudes are shared by authors like Alejo Carpentier, García Márquez, and José Donoso,[8] all of whom tamper with our received ideas of history and, like Conrad, invent imaginary lands where they present their theories of history. All of these writers have contributed ironic chapters to the history of literary utopias, especially insofar as utopias are set, as they have been since More, in the Americas.

If we read *Nostromo* as a parodic utopia, we see that "Conrad's supreme triumph in the evocation of exotic life and colour" (Leavis, pp.231-32) is a feat of illusory realism, that the setting holds up a moral mirror to Europe and is not necesssarily a recreation of the exotic. We are back on Caliban's island, but it is no longer a theater of marvels; now it is merely the scene of sordid capitalist exploitation.

In *Nostromo*, it is not Prospero's magic but the American millionaire Holroyd (or "holy rood," the grotesque cross of evangelical capitalism) and his money that bring Conrad's imaginary Costaguana out of its pastoral torpor. The precapitalist territory has a history but it is cyclical rather than linear, a history of violence that begins with the Spanish *conquistadores* who discover silver and enslave Indians to mine it. The rule of the Spaniards is broken in the wars of independence, but the ideals of leaders like Simón Bolívar—whose lamentations about the "ungovernable" nature of Spanish America are quoted in *Nostromo* (pt. 2, chap. 5, p.161)—disintegrate during chaotic internecine struggles. Spanish American history after liberation is a series of civil wars in which opposing parties fight merely for power and from which the people receive no benefit. Order in that world is synonymous with control, and violence is the customary method either to maintain control or to overthrow it. The intention of the political idealists in that community is to end the history of cyclical repetition and to create a linear history like that of Europe, a history of evolving institutions.

This idealism in personified in *Nostromo* on the political and the economic levels by José Avellanos and Charles Gould. Both weave elaborate fictions in order to explain their motives: Avellanos, a victim—almost a martyr—of the tyranny of Guzman Bento, is an aristocratic "constitutionalist." Which means, simply, that he is committed to peace at home and to business done in a businesslike way abroad. His thoughts on Costaguanan history are in his book *Fifty Years of Misrule* (or *History of Misrule*—it seems to have both titles), which deals with the government of Guzman Bento.[9] The text tells what was wrong with Costaguana and proposes a plan of action that would at least guarantee domestic tranquility. Conrad never gives the details of don José's ideas on government because he wants them to remain vague. Don José is a pathetic fugure in the novel, a man who sacrifices himself to a shapeless ideal that corresponds in no way to the everyday reality of Costaguana. The reader learns nothing about his ideas except that the current regime gives him "a specific mandate to establish the prosperity of the people on the basis of firm peace at home, and to redeem the national credit by the satisfaction of all just claims abroad" (p.126). A "firm peace" implies a free hand for repression, just as the order "to redeem the national credit" suggests paying the exorbitant interest rates demanded by international financiers. His only reality, ultimately, is his book, a martyrology written by a martyr; his government is no government, just a benign form of business-as-usual.

Charles Gould, holder of the Gould Concession, the right to work the silver mine that lies at the heart of *Nostromo*, is a more complex figure than don José Avellanos. He inherits the Concession, a kind of albatross, from his father, who urges him to abandon it. But Gould, despite his father's warning or because of it, decides to restart the mining operations halted during Guzman Bento's regime. Why he does this is mysterious, although it may be part of an Oedipal, fathers-against-sons pattern that reappears throughout the text: Gould senior fails at running the mine, so Gould the son may outdo his father and recover his lost dignity. This possibility is barely mentioned in the novel, although in part 1, chapter 6, upon learning of his father's death, Gould remarks that it was the mine that killed him, but that it might not have, "if he had only grappled with it in a proper way!" (p.63).

The posthumous victory of the son is veiled in the kind of pious public spirit that don José Avellanos expresses. Gould senior was a martyr to Latin America's history, which he called "the appalling darkness of intrigue, bloodshed, and crime that hung over the Queen of Continents" (p.81). Conrad readers will instantly react to the word "darkness" in this context, the chaos that lies just under the surface of civilization as we know it, a darkness a militant West seeks to eradicate, although "the benign project of civilizing the dark places of the world becomes the conscious desire to annihilate everything which opposes man's absolute will."[10] Charles Gould, responding to his father's laments, presents this idealized vision of why he intends to reopen the mine:

What is wanted here is law, good faith, order, security. Anyone can declaim about these things, but I pin my faith to material interests. Only let the material interests once get a firm footing, and they are bound to impose the conditions on which alone they can continue to exist. That's how your money—making is justified here in the face of lawlessness and disorder. It is justified because the security which it demands must be shared with an oppressed people. A better justice will come afterwards. That's your ray of hope. (p.81)

Gould clearly envisions himself as a stage in a process: He will bring Costaguana out of its cycles of rebellion and tyranny into the history of evolving institutions. The idea sounds fine, but it involves some questionable actions, especially the subordination of liberty to the security that "money-making" demands and the hint that the "better justice" to come may be indefinitely postponed.

Conrad wonders at what point the "material interests" become an end instead of a means, at what point Gould will become another Kurtz. This is the central issue of the novel, namely, that the subordination of all things to material interests is a form of economic barbarism and that the power that grows out of the accumulation of material wealth is an irresistible temptation. Thus the silver mine that lies at the heart of the text, the reason why international capitalism, personified by the American Holroyd, extends its tentacles to Costaguana, is merely a symbol. It represents material interests, which, when linked to an international market economy, turn even Western history into a struggle for power. The barbarism Gould and Avellanos want to extirpate returns in a different guise: Instead of the cycles of tyranny and revolt, the new history will be the enslavement of all to the ego of one—Holroyd.

Holroyd is the "hidden god" of *Nostromo*, the first cause for whom Charles Gould is the efficient cause. He represents for Conrad a force that transcends both the idea of history as it is in Costaguana's cyclical mode and in the evolutionary mode as it was envisioned by Hegel. He is Marx's notion of capitalism as the progressive concentration of power and wealth in fewer and fewer hands. Holroyd is the United States, carving out an empire in the twentieth century without having to resort to military force. Holroyd knows the history of European colonialism and views it as a lost cause. His assessment of Europe's folly and the ultimate triumph of the United States as a colonial force is one of the most-often quoted passages in *Nostromo:*

The Costaguana Government shall play its hand for all it's worth—and don't you forget it, Mr. Gould. Now, what is Costaguana? It is the bottomless pit of ten-per-cent loans and other fool investments. European capital had been flung into it with both hands for years. Not ours, though. We in this country know just about enough to keep indoors when it rains. We can sit and watch. Of course, some day we shall step in. We are bound to. But there's no hurry. Time itself has got to wait on the greatest country in the whole of God's Universe. We shall be giving the word for everything: industry, trade, law, journalism, art, politics, and religion, from Cape Horn clear over to Smith's Sound, and beyond, too, if anything worth taking hold of turns up at the North Pole. And then we shall have the leisure to take in hand the outlying islands and continents of the earth. We shall run the world's business whether the world like it or not. The world can't help it—and neither can we, I guess. (p.75)

Beyond Holroyd's bravado, there is a notion here that influences the shaping of *Nostromo*, an idea of history that becomes the shape of this book.

Because it uses an imaginary setting and because it subordinates the development of character to the presentation of ideas, *Nostromo* ought to be read as a satiric utopia. Costaguana, even though it is a composite of many Spanish American nineteenth-century republics, is a "no-place," a mirror held up, not to an exotic "other world," but to the prevailing situation of the West. International capitalism, the "material interests" alluded to so often in the text, recognizes no national boundaries. Holroyd is an American who understands the role the United States is destined to play in the coming phase of international "development," but even he recognizes that he is part of a process that has its own ontogeny. Holroyd is a species of "world-historical-figure," the embodiment of the principles he enunciates in the passage quoted above.

At the same time he postulates this deterministic view of history, Conrad argues that individuals can retain some degree of independence. In fact, the human

drama of the novel (as opposed to the inhuman or superhuman drama of international capitalism) deals precisely with the notion of fidelity to self. Throughout
his writings, Conrad classifies his characters according
to their ability to live out the destinies they create—as
the writer himself fashions destinies—for themselves:
There are the MacWhirrs (*Typhoon*) who are what they
do, individuals Conrad admires even if he relegates
them to a lower rank, and the Lord Jims, whose relation to their professions is less fixed and who, because
of their crises and changes, are more interesting psychologically.

In *Nostromo*, Captain Mitchell is of the MacWhirr
type, as is the "Garibaldino," Giorgio Viola, both men
of principle who never doubt their principles. Their
tenacity enables them to survive, just as their blind-
ness to anything but duty creates an irony: Their an-
gelic perfection makes them fools. The burden of the
more psychologically complex characters is being
aware of that irony, of experiencing a destructive type
of *desenqaño* or loss of illusion. This experience, a major theme of the Spanish-speaking world in the seventeenth century, was originally religious in nature: The
"man of the world" would awaken one day to his folly;
the scales would fall from his eyes, and he would see
the illusions of this world for what they are. He would
then fix his sight on salvation and the next world.
Conrad's *desengaño* is secular, an existential collapse
whose most radical form destroys the skeptic Decoud.

Conrad's characters all need fictions in which to believe because the fiction and the believing—acts both
in the sense of actions and in the sense of part-play-
ing—make human life possible. As Alan Sandison
says, this fidelity to oneself may be selfish, "but in preserving oneself one is preserving others."[11] This would
seem to make Conrad into a precursor of Camus and
other Existentialists, and in his concern for the integ-

rity of the self and its continued existence in the face of doubt he does resemble them. This maintenance of the self through an act of will is Romantic in origin, and is one of the most heavily used themes in twentieth-century Western literature, both in tragic and comic plots and in ironic and nonironic narratives.

In *Nostromo*, Conrad subordinates that important theme to a meditation on history, and this subordination explains some of the novel's irony as well as its structure—which so many critics have found faulty. Eloise Knapp Hay's complaints (quoted above) about the "disorderly presentation of material" in part 1 of the novel and the seeming lack of "human interest—the only worthy interest in a novel" represent the general critical verdict on *Nostromo:* It is a great but flawed novel. A demurring point of view might counter that Conrad in all likelihood knew what he was doing when he wrote *Nostromo* and that his methods in part 1 might be a signal to the reader about how he wanted his book to be read.

A much later text, Garcia Máquez's *One Hundred Years of Solitude* (1967), illuminates Conrad's strategy. The first sentence of García Márquez's satiric romance refers to no discerible present moment, and alludes to events already transpired but not yet narrated: "Many years later, before the firing squad, Colonel Aureliano Buendia was to remember the day his father took him to see ice." García Márquez in this way gives the reader "memories" of the future: When an event takes place, it fulfills a prophecy made earlier in the book. The effect is the reduction of the chronological and sequential aspects of the text to a single point, as if the reader could experience the whole text simultaneously in spatial terms instead of bit by bit, in chronological order. The reader thus gets the same perspective on the whole the writer has as he produces the work.

In part 1 of *Nostromo*, "The Silver of the Mine,"

Conrad deliberately confuses the chronology of his story so that the reader will not know what is happening
"now" or has already taken place. In chapter 2, Conrad
introduces Captain Mitchell, a man absolutely committed to his work, totally competent and devoid of
imagination. As if to contrast the orderly nature of
Captain Mitchell with the chaos of Costaguana politics, Conrad tells an anecdote using Mitchell as a
point of view: "On a memorable occasion he [Mitchell]
had been called upon to save the life of a dictator. . . .
Poor Señor Ribiera (such was the dictator's name) had
come pelting eighty miles over mountain tracks after
the lost battle of Socorro . . ." (p.23). At this point in
the novel, the reader can have no idea of the importance of this anecdote nor of its relative position with
regard to the "now" in which the narrative is set. What
seems a casual anecdote is the climax of the text, the
revolution that threatens to bring down the government, take the silver mine away from Gould, and
sweep the country back into chaos. As we read "away"
from Mitchell's anecdote, we read "towards" it in
terms of the work's chronology and in terms of the
number of pages we have to read to reach it. The "line"
of the narrative, of course, twists in the process into a
circle.

Readers of *One Hundred Years of Solitude* will recognize this narrative prestidigitation. They will recall
how García Márquez constantly plays with the linear
experience of reading by implanting memories of events
to come in their minds. The result, both in *Nostromo*
and *One Hundred years of Solitude,* is the turning of
time into space. Jocelyn Baines defines the effects of
Conrad's manipulation of narrative time in this way:

The effect of these time shifts is almost to abolish
time in *Nostromo*. The elimination of progression
from one event to another also has the effect of imply-
ing that nothing is ever achieved. By the end of the

book we are virtually back where we started; it looks as if the future of Costaguana will be very similar to her past.[12]

Nostromo is a desperate text and its desperation reappears in authors like Alejo Carpentier (in his *The Kingdom of this World*) and in García Márquez (in his *One Hundred Years of Solitude*). These writers take Conrad's despair—each clash of wills brings violence and bloodshed—to the point of a deathwish. Both Carpentier and García Márquez conjure up hurricanes (García Márquez's clearly inspired by Carpentier's) to blow their created worlds into oblivion, to turn each of them into a *tabula rasa* where history can be inscribed anew. Conrad, Carpentier, and García Márquez all echo Stephen Dedalus's complaint ("History is a nightmare from which I am trying to awake"), but none succeeds in transforming the nightmare into the utopian dream because all remain faithful to the real evidence of history before them.

It has fallen to José Donoso to take a first step towards accomplishing that task, a step he takes without turning his fiction into a utopia totally disconnected from reality. His *A House in the Country* shows how the cycles of revolution and repression, of the triumph of material interests may be broken: The drama of his text is tragic because his utopia is crushed, but it does inscribe the possibility of a new day, a new history, at least for Spanish America.

Like *Nostromo* and *One Hundred Years of Solitude*, *A House in the Country* is set in an imaginary land, during a vague period when horses have not yet been replaced by automobiles. And like the two earlier texts, *A House in the Country* deals with the colonial situation from the point of view of the *criollos*, those born in the country of European descent, with no Indian or negro ancestors. The *criollo* aspect of *Nostromo* is often overlooked by English and American readers: Charles Gould, while of English "blood," thinks himself a native of Costaguana, with as much right to act in order to change its history as any of its mixed-blood dictators.

A House in the Country also deals with *criollos*, not, like Charles Gould, of English ancestry, but those Conrad describes in *Nostromo* in this way: "the great owners of estates on the plain, grave, courteous, simple men, *caballeros* of pure descent, with small hands and feet, conservative, hospitable, and kind" (p.41). The manners of the Venturas, the *criollo* family Donoso scrutinizes in his novel, do not coincide exactly with Conrad's description, but they nevertheless consider themselves an elite, superior in nature to those around them. Their mere existence is, for them, proof that God himself intended them for their position in the world.

There are myriad Venturas, and their wealth, like that of the Goulds, derives from a mine. But unlike Charles Gould, who imagines himself a transitional figure in Costaguanan history—"material interests" would provide stability, which in turn would cause the people to renounce disorder and misrule—the Venturas are resolute defenders of the status quo. They subscribe to a doctrine similar to the divine right of kings and countenance no questioning of their authority. Thus, while Charles Gould deludes himself into thinking he can use self-interest to better his country, the Venturas believe that material interests and the nation itself exist in order to provide them with an income and servants. In both novels, blind egoism leads to calamity.

Where Conrad and Donoso differ is their attitude towards the dynamics of history. Conrad sees a difference between the first two periods of Costaguanan history, Spanish rule and anarchic independence, as primitive variations of what was to come: The Spanish *conquistadores* work the silver mine with slave labor; during independence, with the mine under English control, it becomes a convenient symbol of foreign intervention and imperialism. In the third phase of Costaguanan history, the mine becomes Costaguana's link to international capitalism, a symbol of the subordination of all human life to material interests. Conrad denounces this situation because it breeds future violence, which will come when the socialists and communists of his final chapter triumph over the Goulds. He is not pleased with this prospect, and the despair in his text results from his not seeing any escape from material interests except violence.

Donoso agrees, but sees this violence as necessary because it would eliminate the very basis of the Venturas' wealth and the subordination of human life to things. The revolution he envisions would abolish private property. This utopian aspect of Donoso's novel is an echo of Don Quijote's discourse to the goatherds (*Don Quijote*, bk. 1, chap. 11), where Don Quijote praises the golden age in which the words "yours" and "mine" did not exist. Cervantes may have intended this speech as a mockery of utopian schemes, but it does evoke the radical critiques of private property made by Christian humanists, especially Thomas More. Donoso's utopian attack on private ownership requires the reader to recall similar attacks made during the eighteenth century by Rousseau, and in the nineteenth century by Pierre Joseph Proudhon, which were later systematized by Marx and Engels. The gold of the mine in *A House in the Country* conjures up golden ages, the idealized past, the utopian present, and the *real* future predicted by Marx and Engels, all golden ages in which, paradoxically, gold would have no value.

Donoso's text chronicles a critical moment in the Ventura family history, one in which their concept of history as repetition and perpetual present suffers a shock. This shock derives precisely from the criticism of private property that has been a constant though subterranean current in Western thought since antiquity, a criticism that seeks, especially in the analysis of Marx and Engels, to prove that private property is a fiction and not a reality. Marx and Engels say that society, ours or the Venturas', is as it is because we assume private property to be a "fact of life":

Property owners and proletarians evince the same human self-alienation. But the landowners find in this self-alienation their confirmation and their good, their power: In it they have the appearance of human existence. The proletarians feel annihilated in their self-alienation; it they see their impotence and the reality of an inhuman existence.[13]

The Venturas justify their ownership of property by having recourse to tradition. Their ancestors took control of the mine and the natives (Donoso never refers to them as Indians, thus preserving the abstract nature of those oppressed) who work it. The natives turn the gold they mine into gold leaf, which they give to the Venturas in exchange for goods worth very little relative to the market value of the gold leaf. The Venturas sell the gold leaf to foreigners, transforming it into money and the power it creates. Their defense of this primitive colonialism, aside from their idea that since things have "always" been this way they must be right, is based on a differentiation they make between themselves and the natives.

Tradition says the natives are cannibals—although the Venturas have supposedly purged the active exercise of this vice out of them. Cannibals, according to the "authorities" that lie at the basis of the Spaniards' justification for the conquest of the New World, are not human because human beings, by definition, do not eat their own kind. Since the natives are not human, it is both legal and laudable to enslave them. This postulate, mocked during the Renaissance by Montaigne in his essay on the cannibals, is nothing more than a fiction engendered by the idea of private property. Once private property is taken as a fact it creates its own defenses—the enslavement of supposed cannibals is one example—and these defenses become an ideology and a morality: Since history and tradition support these customs, they must, according to the Venturas, be sanctioned by God himself. Any alteration of them would not only be treason but heresy as well.

Private property thus produces an order, a social structure: The Venturas are the apex and the natives the base of the social triangle. The intermediate classes are composed of two groups, the family servants, who are superior to the natives but who lack individual identity for the Venturas, and the Ventura children, Venturas *in potentia* but not yet Venturas. The servants constitute a private army, whose mission, aside from attending to the needs of the Venturas themselves, is to keep the Ventura children under surveillance. As Lidia, the Ventura who administers the staff, puts it each year in her address to new servants:

These [children], she assured them in her harangue, were their enemies, intent on their destruction because they wanted to destroy everything stable by their questioning of rules. Let the servants be aware of the brutishness of beings who, because they were still children, had not yet acceded to the illuminated class of their elders, and were capable of anything with their abuse, their disobedience, their filth, their demands, their destruction, attacks, undermining of peace and order by means of criticism and doubt. They were fully capable of annihilating them, the servants, for being the guardians, exactly so, of this civilized order, which was so venerable it defied all criticism. The danger of the children was only inferior to that of the cannibals, of whom it was not impossible that they, the children, ignorant as they were and perhaps in no ill-intentioned way, might even unwittingly be the agents. (pp. 40-41)

Similar to the children are the in-laws, necessary for the perpetuation of the family but not really part of it; it is a alliance of one in-law, some children, and some natives that threatens the Venturas' "civilized order."

The servants are another kind of threat: As long as they remain servants or serve as a police force to spy upon and keep order among the children, they are mere projections of the Venturas' will. But armed and imbued with a sense of mission, what one of the Venturas calls "the mystical code that has guided our family since time immemorial" (p.269), they do indeed become a menace. When they identify themselves totally with the values of the Venturas, they find they have something they did not have before, an identity and a role in history. The instant they make that discovery the Venturas become expendable because the values they inculcate into their servants are greater than the Venturas themselves. And the moment the Venturas show the slightest weakness or indecision, the servants realize that only they are pure enough to be the keepers of that great tradition.

Donoso's drama, the abortive revolution against personal property, is more obviously allegorical than Conrad's meditation on material interests in *Nostromo*. Conrad deals with the inhuman history of things—the international economy—and how human beings are incorporated into it. Readers expecting to find a human drama (or melodrama) are frustrated because they find a disordered, oblique story whose protagonist dies in an absurd confusion of identity. Donoso alienates his reader in quite a different fashion: He puts his reader on guard from the outset by constantly intervening in the narrative in his own voice just to remind the reader that his book is indeed a fiction. This authorial interruption is related to the concept of personal property at an aesthetic level, but its main effect is to destroy sentimental lines between reader and character, or any notion that *A House in the Country* is a portrait of life.

The allegorical possibilites in *A House in the Country* are immense precisely because Donoso constantly reminds us that the text is a fiction. We can read it, for example, as an allegory on the history of Chile, Donoso's homeland, at the time of the coup against Salvador Allende in 1973. In the novel, the adult Venturas and their servants go off on an excursion and leave their children alone in the huge summer house. The trip is to last a day, but it is extended magically into an entire year. The Venturas' decision to absent themselves could correspond to the free elections that brought Allende to power, a moment in which neither the Venturas (the oligarchic upper classes) nor their servants (the armed forces) chose to intervene in national politics.

Suddenly a leader appears: In the novel this is the supposedly man brother-in-law Adriano Gomara, a physician known for his benevolence towards the natives (the lowest classes). Adriano Gomara emerges as a leader because he can mediate between the various factions that materialize among the Ventura children and the natives. His improvised government collapses because he cannot control the more radical elements within the ranks of the children and natives and because he cannot match the violent repression that takes place when the Venturas send their servants back to the country house to reassert their values and to repossess their property.

The Venturas' attempt to reverse history fails: One

of the Ventura children, Malvina, forms an alliance with the foreigners who buy the gold leaf as a first step in taking possession of the mine. The Venturas are doomed, just as the utopian project of Adriano Gomara to forge a society without private property is doomed, but the history is redefined as a linear, irreversible process of change. No system is permanent, not even that of the Venturas. Donoso ultimately resolves nothing. Like Alejo Carpentier and García Márquez he ends his text with a natural disaster, one that wipes out the adult Venturas. The surviving children remain in the summer house while the servants, Malvina, and the foreigners escape to the city. The reader may wonder whether the surviving children will form the nucleus of a revolutionary avant-garde, but Donoso refuses to feed any speculation, rejecting the idea of projecting the novel beyond its limits. This is the chronicle of the fall of the Venturas, but their world, the world of private property, continues to exist without them.

Throughout the text, Donoso struggles against the idea of the representational in literature: His constant intervention in the book, his insistence on speaking as the author and not merely as a narrator, his commentary on the progression of the plot, are all devices he uses to keep the reader from confusing art and life. In the second chapter, Donoso explains to a reader he imagines growing impatient with his authorial interruptions that:

I do it with the modest goal of suggesting that the reader accept what I write as artifice. When I intervene from time to time in the story, I only do so in order to remind the reader of his distance from the material of this novel, a thing I want to keep as my own object, one I show, display, but never relinquish completely so the reader may confuse his own experience with it. If I succeed in getting the public to accept these authorial manipulations, they will recognize not only that distance but also the fact that the old narrative devices, so discredited these days, may produce results as substantial as those created by conventions dissimulated by "good taste" and its hidden arsenal of tricks. (p.53)

Here we see Donoso wrestling with a phantom that has haunted him since his earliest publications, the legacy of Realism. Donoso found his place in the literary tradition by means of parody, especialy the parody of the Chilean novel of *costumbrista* tendency, with its minute depiction of Chilean life. Here he integrates his parodic literary personality with the central theme of his novel, private property. In the passage above he states that he does not, want the reader to identify himself with the characters, but he does not thwart this identification by means of some Brechtian "alienation effect." For Donoso, the traditional novel was aesthetically valid and, moreover, better as fiction than the contemporary novel, the French New Novel for example. That is, the obvious display of devices in a novel by Balzac or Trollope reminds today's readers they are reading a work of art and that they must not allow themselves to rework the text into their own image as they might be tempted to do with the kind of text that invites the reader to be a co-creator or literary accomplice. Donoso is also doing it because he wants to remind the reader that this book belongs to José Donoso.

He expresses the same possessive spirit at the end of the novel, when the narrator explains why it is so difficult for him to end the book:

It's curious nevertheless—and this is the point I wanted to make—that even though I've made my characters non-psychlogical, unrealistic, and artificial, I have not been able to avoid connecting myself to them emotionally and to their world, from which it would be as impossible to separate them as it would be to separate, for example, one of Ucello's hunters from his meadow he crosses. In other words, despite my determination not to mix reality and art, it's terribly painful for me to say this farewell, a conflict that takes the literary form of my not wanting to leave them behind without finishing *their* stories—forgetting that they have no more or less of a story than the one I want to give them—instead of settling for finishing *this* story which, in some way I don't fully understand, is, no doubt of it, my own. (p.492)

After reading these two passages it is impossible not to think of Jorge Luis Borges. The same desire to rebel against the idea that literature is a mirror held up to life, the same desire to make the literary text a work of art that should be enjoyed for itself and not for its fidelity to the real world—even Donoso's use of the word "artifice" reminds us that Borges called the second group of stories in *Ficciones* "Artifices"—all of this delineates the problems involved in being a writer in the twentieth century. Conrad ran great risks in *Nostromo* by constructing a text he knew would confound readers accustomed to nineteenth-century storytelling, readers used to psychologically complex main characters and stereotyped secondary characters. By diverting attention away from character toward structure, Conrad broke with his immediate tradition and revitalized the novel of ideas, whose origins lie in satire.

Donoso's dilemma as a late twentieth-century writer is that he wants to do something similar to what Conrad did—meditate on the relationship between things and people in an imaginary land—but he cannot separate that meditation from a self-conscious contemplation of himself as a writer producing such a text. The example of Milton trying to write an epic poem and feeling obliged to take into account not only the classical and Renaissance epic traditions but also any knowledge even vaguely related to his subject (sunspots for example) comes to mind: The more self-conscious the text becomes, the more complex the materials the artist feels obliged to manipulate grow, and the more the resultant text becomes the writer's projected self-image, his metaphoric autobiography. Like the man Borges describes at the end of *El Hacedor* (The Maker), who proposes to draw a map of the world only to discover after years of labor that he has succeeded in drawing a self-portrait, Donoso (and Borges) finds that he is his text.

The image of Mary Shelley's monster in *Frankenstein; or, the Modern Prometheus*[14] also comes to mind here: Frankenstein is a type for the artist who creates his work of art from the *disjecta membra* of tradition. The final product is not only monstrous, an involuntary caricature—what the Romantic artist always fears he will engender—but a monstrous double of the artist himself. Where the Romantic would attempt to save face by blaming his medium—language—for its incapacity to express his intuitions, the modern artist cannot shift responsibility for the monstrous nature of his text away from himself. The Romantic at least possesses an ego he wishes he could express and communicate to others; the modern writer ambiguously finds his self-justification in the act of writing. His published text is monstrous because it makes many demands on him—aesthetic, political, social—and is simultaneously a mirror in which he sees his own confused self-image.

To publish that self-image is precisely to disconnect it from the self, to send it into the world where, like Frankenstein's monster, it will take on other identities even as it usurps its creator's name. Loss of name is a loss of identity, and personal identity is one kind of personal property Donoso has great difficulty criticizing. This is in fact a theme that reappears throughout

Donoso's writing, with great poignancy in *The Obscene Bird of Night*, where the failed author Humberto Peñaloza vainly tries to recover all the copies of his only book because its mere existence in someone else's library constitutes a loss of identity. Publication as loss of identity is the twentieth century's peculiar and ironic contribution to the *topos* of writing as a means to achieve fame and immortality. For writers like Borges and Donoso, writing is a kind of affliction that ultimately renders the author anonymous.

Thus, the issue of private property has the same value in *A House in the Country* that the idea of material interests has in *Nostromo.* The difference lies in the degree of self-consciousness, the degree to which the author of each text wants to put himself as author on display before the reader. *Nostromo* stands at the beginning of the modern tradition because of its deliberate alienation of the reader who comes to the novel hoping to identify with its central character. *A House in the Country* continues that tradition of putting the mechanisms of the text on display the better to explore the possibilities of the subject. The example of Thackeray in *Vanity Fair*, with its famous concluding passage about the characters who seem so real being mere puppets the author-narrator now puts back into their box, provides some idea of how venerable this tradition of allegorical novel-writing is.

This is not simply to say that the novel incorporates an earlier satiric or allegorical tradition into itself—even if this is obviously true—but to demonstrate that the tradition of true-to-life characters, the creation of novels in which the reader is invited to identify himself with the characters, while dominant over a long period of the novel's history, is not the only novelistic tradition. At the same time, Donoso's remarks above (pp.82-83) point out that more than verisimilitude is involved in the creation of character: The author takes a proprietary interest in his characters because they are his creation, because in some way they reflect him. This is a different sort of sentimental relationship from that of the reader who identifies himself with a character, but the possessive aspects are the same.

This situation, in which the author asserts his rights over the text, dramatizes the problem of literary meaning. Not only will the author lose his identity through writing but he will also lose exclusive rights over the text, as it becomes a part of the literary tradition, something with its own meaning-producing devices. No matter how much the author-in-the-text may protest, the literary text after publication is no longer his: It becomes part of the tradition and part of every reader's experience. In every way, it resembles the summer house Donoso uses as the center of his novel: The Venturas erected the house as a monument to themselves, to their power. It is surrounded by a fence made of iron lances that separates it from the rest of the world and marks it as personal, private property. When the children, the natives, and Adriano Gomara take control of the house, they take away the fence, symbolically destroying the idea of the house as personal property.

The restoration effected by the servants produces a parody of the earlier situation: Once an object is inserted in time, it becomes part of time and changes. This principle may be applied to society itself as well as to the work of art once it leaves the artist's hands. The author-in-the-text is part of the text: His asides to the reader are part of the text and are therefore public property. The author, like Frankenstein, possesses his text only as long as he refrains from redacting it; from then on it belongs to no one or anyone.

Like Conrad, Donoso reveals a horrifying reality to us without resolving it in any way. There is no escape from material interests, just as there is no escape from the delusion of personal property or individual identity. Both *Nostromo* and *A House in the Country* parody the Realist tradition, which they both admire, but which requires a worldview unacceptable to both. These are not revolutionary novels in the political sense, but they are apocalyptic texts that prefer to announce the death of an old tradition rather than the birth of a new one.

3

The Novel of Persecution: From William Godwin to Reinaldo Arenas

That the novel of persecution, the chronicle of a flight from real or imaginary enemies (political or personal) and the novel of the artist's life should in many cases be one and the same text is the legacy of Romanticism. Since the Romantic era, Western culture has been concerned with the idiosyncrasies of the individual, especially of those individuals—artists and political leaders—qualitatively different from the rest of humanity (declared politically equal by the Enlightenment). These two groups, especially since the French Revolution and the rise of Napoleon, are essential to human societies and yet outside them, as if the special talents of the great should make them taboo. The Romantic hero, typically, is a solitary, isolated from his followers, misunderstood, often mad or visionary, and the Romantic artist follows suit. For this reason the Wandering Jew or the Ancient Mariner, Victor Hugo in exile, Napoleon on St. Helena, or Edgar Allan Poe adrift in the United States have become images that haunt the imagination of our own century.

The hero and the artist lack a fixed abode in post-Romantic culture and are the perennial targets of the guardians of the status quo. The friction between artists and critics mirrors the relationship between radicals and governments that often culminates in violence and repression. One result of this violence, when society rejects revolutionary art or politics, is the real or metaphoric imprisonment of these eccentrics. Imprisoned, the artist or political activist strives to remind himself of the freedom of his soul, mind, or imagination and seeks to record his experience through writing. Writing thus becomes the last refuge of the fugitive or the prisoner and his text the only place where he can be truly free. As Victor Brombert has shown,[1] the Romantics transformed the picture of the incarcerated artist (the mad Tasso for example) into a metaphor of the artist at work: Like a monk, he transforms his cell into a world where he is "a master of infinite space."

The fugitive or prisoner's escape into the freedom of writing despite his being harassed or locked up is a theme that links two texts divided by one hundred and fifty years of history: William Godwin's *Things as They Are; or the Adventures of Caleb Williams* (1794)[2] and Reinaldo Arenas's *El mundo alucinante (una novela de aventuras)* (1969) (The Hallucinating World [a novel of adventures]).[3] These seemingly disparate books, one the product of the twilight of the Enlightenment, the other the product of the regime of Fidel Castro's Cuba, are united by more than theme. Both are romances, as the word "adventures" in both titles suggests.

Jorge Luis Borges, in his preface to Adolfo Bioy Casares's novella *La invención de Morel* (1940) *(The Invention of Morel)*[4] seeks to dignify romance, which he calls the "novela de peripecias" or "novela de aventuras" (novel of peripeteia or adventures). Borges declares that the psychological or realist novel tends to be shapeless because it attempts to copy real life, itself devoid of pattern. The adventure novel, he adds, recognizes its own artificiality, its identity as a work of art instead of transcription or redaction of life. Because it is grounded in art, the adventure novel allows no extraneous elements, no descriptions of states of mind, no gratuitous landscape or urban descriptions unless they come to the point of the plot. Readers of romances or adventure novels may demur at this point, especially if they recall Cervantes's criticism of the romances of chivalry: Through don Quijote, Cervantes attacks these primordial romances because, like the picaresque satires of the sixteenth century, they are episodic, devoid of the well-organized plot Borges claims to be the essence of the adventure novel. Borges's attacks on the novel should not be taken too seriously—he is defending one kind of fiction and therefore feels obliged to attack another, which he sees as a rival—but what he says about romance's swerve away from realism and its achieving a unity unrelated to psychology are ideas that demand scrutiny.

In *The Secular Scripture*,[5] Northrop Frye defends romance in a way that complements Borges's attacks on the vagaries of the psychological novel. Frye points out that romance, with its fairy-tale plots, is able to re-enact archetypal plots, the myths of a given society, in a way the novel, bound to history and psychology, cannot. Romance succeeds precisely because of what its detractors see as its principal defect, its all-too-obvious apparatus, its unabashed use of retarding devices such as the interpolated tale, loss of identity, and, of course, recognition scenes. Satiric writers like Cervantes or Fielding have always parodied the devices of romance but it is clear that the novel, especially in the nineteenth century—*Wuthering Heights, Great Expectations,* or *Moby Dick* are examples—could not survive without incorporating romance elements. Parody then has actually helped to save the very thing it seems intent on eradicating.

In fact, the use of romance structures in satire is one of the hallmarks of the literature of the twentieth century, particularly its constant reuse of the quest plot.

Authors as different as Gide, Thomas Pynchon, Kafka, and Henry Miller have set their protagonists on the road to self-discovery only to have them stumble into the slough of *desenqaño* or end up, like the protagonists of Céline or Cortázar, in the madhouse. These texts move between comic satire, in which the foibles of society are ridiculed, to ironic satires, in which the grim absurdity of man's fate is revealed in all its horror. All of these fictions use the elastic yet curiously rigorous structure of romance, especially in the form of the first-person confessional narrative.

Of particular relevance to this comparative study of William Godwin and Reinaldo Arenas is Virginia Woolf's experiment in imaginary biography, *Orlando* (1928). This text, which traces the female artist's quest for identity by following her escape from the limitations imposed on her my male-dominated society, defines writing as the only escape from a life that is a kind of prison. *Orlando* mediates between Godwin and Arenas in a transition that attenuates the heavy melodrama of *Caleb Williams* by means of fantasy, fantasy that reaches surreal heights in Arenas. Thus we shall be comparing Godwin's forthright use of romance structures to depict "things as they are" with Arenas's satiric use of romance structures to show writing to be an escape from the unreal world of political persecution. It is Woolf's *Orlando* that enables Arenas to make his point, and he pays homage to her by incorporating her Orlando into his book.

Unlike *Orlando* or *El mundo alucinante, Caleb Williams* is not usually read as literature but as a literary dramatization of Godwin's *Enquiry Concerning Political Justice* (1793), much in the way *Emile* is read as a compendium of Rousseau's thoughts on education. Godwin certainly had Rousseau's text in mind when he wrote *Caleb Williams,* and his romance certainly does dramatize the ideas in the *Enquiry*. It is equally true that Godwin's book has survived as a fiction in its own right. That is, the justification for the book's existence is not the author's political theories but its literary merits, its having engendered a long line of persecution narratives. Thus, in order to read *Caleb Williams* as literature it is not to his philosophic writings that we ought to turn but to other literary texts, specifically to Cervantes's *Don Quijote.*

Cervantes's protagonists are an *hidalgo* gone mad because he has read too many romances of chivalry and a peasant, sane but gullible enough to be moved by his master's fantastic rhetoric. The comic play of appearance and reality, illusion and substance, literature and life, dominates Part I of the *Quijote,* where there is genuine criticism of romances of chivalry both as literary works of art and as evil influences on readers. Godwin seems to have taken to heart Cervantes's criticism of the code of chivalry as that code is presented in the chivalric novel because he makes the reading of romances and the influence of the chivalric code on his characters the source of their disasters.

Whereas Cervantes's central characters are comic opposites, Godwin's Caleb Williams and Mr. Falkland, the servant and the master, are mirror images of each other. They are socially and economically different, but they are ultimately the same person, formed and deformed by having read the same books. At the beginning of his story, Caleb reveals his "tragic flaw":

The spring of action which, perhaps more than any other, characterised the whole train of my life, was curiosity. It was this that gave me my mechanical turn; I was desirous of tracing the variety of effects which might be produced from given causes. It was this that made me a sort of natural philosopher; I could not rest till I had acquainted myself with the solutions that had been invented for the phenomena of the universe. In fine, this produced in me an

invincible attachment to books of narrative and romance. I panted for the unravelling of an adventure,
with an anxiety, perhaps almost equal to that of the
man whose future happiness or misery depended on
its issue. I read, I devoured compositions of this sort.
They took possession of my soul; and the effects they
produced, were frequently discernible in my external
appearance and my health.(p.4)

This passage, a sketch of both the ideal reader of mystery novels and the detective protagonist of those novels, must be compared with this description, a kind of
interpolated tale, of Mr. Falkland by his old retainer
Collins:

Among the favourite authors of his early years were
the heroic poets of Italy. From them he imbibed the
love of chivalry and romance. He had too much good
sense to regret the times of Charlemagne and Arthur.
But, while his imagination was purged by a certain
infusion of philosophy, he conceived that there was in
the manners depicted by these celebrated poets, something to imitate, as well as something to avoid. He
believed that nothing was so well calculated to make
men delicate, gallant and humane, as a temper perpetually alive to the sentiments of birth and honour.
The opinions he entertained upon these topics were
illustrated in his conduct, which was assiduously con-
formed to the model of heroism that his fancy
suggested. (p.10)

Both passages illustrate Godwin's belief that evil acts
result from faults in education, that, in short, men are
basically good but liable to be perverted by bad books—
especially romances of chivalry which on the one hand
make us sensitive to mystery and melodrama and on
the other make us acutely aware of personal honor.

These parallel passages show that eighteenth-century England read the *Quijote* on several different levels, both literary and nonliterary. (A parallel to God-

win's serious reading of Cervantes as a guide to what books might be dangerous to young minds is Charles Lucas's *The Infernal Quixote* [1800], an attack on Godwin, Locke, Rousseau, and virtually all other "liberal" thinkers of the eighteenth century.) Godwin, like Cervantes's barber and curate, is convinced that Cervantes's message about romances is socially significant, although at the same time he makes literary use of the madness those evil books engender.

In the *Quijote*, Sancho and don Quijote discover they are characters in a comic romance, a discovery that, as Borges has noted, [6] makes the reader question the solidity of his own reality. Like the play-within-a-play in *Hamlet*, this device calls attention to the artificiality of the text by adding yet one more layer of "fiction" to the fiction in progress. Godwin uses the metamorphosis that occurs late in Alonso Quijana's life—his transformation into don Quijote—and makes his chracters go mad early in their lives. Reading, therefore, is not only an educational process but a potential danger to personality: Caleb and Falkland are not merely characters who go mad because of reading but characters who are never really sane. Throughout their lives they are displaced characters (not people) searching for an appropriate fiction, prefigurations of Pirandello's six characters.

Northrop Frye points out that the conclusion of a traditional romance contains a restoration of the protagonist's lost identity, a convention Cervantes twists to his own purpose (to prevent any more sequels) by having don Quijote "die" and Alonso Quijana awaken, as if from a dream—just in time to die. When Frye says, "Identity means a good many things, but all its meanings in romance have some connection with a state of existence in which there is nothing to write about" (*Secular Scripture*, p.54), he reveals why *Caleb Williams* constantly postpones coming to a conclusion.

The book has no real ending, despite the fact that Godwin invented two, because neither Caleb nor his tormentor-double Falkland has any real identity: Both are displaced Quijotes who cannot become Alonso Quijanas.

It is in this matter of the restoration of identity that Godwin deviates most radically from true romance. Death alone can release Falkland from him unending, self-contained chivalric novel. Caleb is denied even this release because his destiny is to become an emblem of the writer, a figure like Samuel Beckett's decrepit narrators who "can't" but "must" go on. In himself, Caleb is nothing; by the end of his narrative he is his writing and nothing more. The process by which Caleb turns into the paradigm of the writer derives from common Renaissance models, especially the picaresque, protean outlaw artist (see chap. 1, n.6, p.82). Like Autolycus in *The Winter's Tale*, Ginés de Pasamonte in the *Quijote*, or Pablos in Quevedo's *Buscón*, Caleb survives because of his ability to disquise himself and thus escape both the law and Falkland's minions. Adrift in the world, he immediately turns to literature to earn a living.

Godwin carefully arranges Caleb's metamorphosis: After he escapes from the jail where Falkland has had him locked up under false charges, Caleb passes himself off as a foreigner, an Irishman; he then becomes the quintessential outsider, a Jew. Godwin clearly intends to evoke the legend of the Wandering Jew, but the devices he uses to increase the melodramatic shifts in Caleb's life oblige us to think of him more in a literary than in an ethical or moral context. Instead of feeling pity for Caleb, condemned like Ahasuerus or Cartaphilus to wander the earth forever, a contemporary reader might be more inclined to see Caleb's life as a series of trials wherein a character whose identity already derives from literature becomes first an artist then art itself.

The process whereby Caleb turns into a text begins before he actually writes. Disguised, making his way to London and total anonymity, he hears stories about himself, the notorious Kit Williams. A woman tells him his own story: "He was as handsome, likely a lad, as any in four counties round; and that she loved him for his cleverness, by which he outwitted all the keepers they could set over him, and made his way through stone walls, as if they were so many cobwebs" (p.237). By the time she has finished, Caleb realizes he has become a mythic *picaro* in popular literature: "I had gained fame indeed, the miserable fame to have my story bawled forth by hawkers and ballad-mongers, to have my praises as an active and enterprising villain celebrated among footmen and chambermaids; but I was neither an Erostratus nor an Alexander, to die contented with that species of eulogium" (p.274). Caleb's decision to tell his own tale may have more to it than the pious purposes he lists when he begins his narrative (to keep himself from despair and to seek justice from posterity): He wants to keep his story to himself.[7]

As an author and a reader, Caleb knows that all authors are thieves and that the hack writer steals in order to survive, disguising himself in someone else's work much as he, Caleb, must disguise himself in other identities. Caleb's literary career gives us some insight into which kinds of literary texts could be commodities and which not: When he begins to write in London, he first tries to publish poetry. He fails: The editor of the newspaper to which he submits his compositions will not pay for them because they will not increase his circulation. Caleb takes the editor's advice: "It was their constant rule to give nothing for poetical compositions, the letter-box being always full of

writings of that sort; but, if the gentleman would try
his hand in prose, a short essay or a tale, he would see
what he could do for him" (p.259). Caleb produces "a
paper in the style of Addison's Spectators, which was
accepted," but realizes the essay is not his true calling:

I however distrusted my resources in this way of moral disquisition, and soon turned my thoughts to his
[the editor's] other suggestion, a tale. His demands
upon me were now frequent, and to facilitate my la-
bour I bethought myself of the resource of
translation. . . . I frequently translated or modelled
my narratives upon a reading of some years before. By
a fatality for which I did not exactly know how to
account, my thoughts frequently led me to the histories of celebrated robbers; and I retailed from time to
time incidents and anecdotes of Cartouche, Gusman
d'Alfarache and other memorable worthies, whose career was terminated upon the gallows or the scaffold.
(p.259)

Like Ginés de Pasamonte in *Don Quijote*, Caleb becomes a picaresque writer specializing in picaresque
narratives. Even in this he is a thief, stealing from
Mateo Alemán in the same way Lesage stole from the
Spanish picaresque tradition to create *Gil Blas*. It is
equally clear that he passes his translations off as original compositions, a kind of theft of stolen goods.

Caleb says little about his writing because it is not as
important to him as two other texts, the one we are
reading and the anonymous *Surprising History of Caleb Williams* that Mr. Falkland uses as a scourge to
keep Caleb from ever settling in any one place—biography as a mark of Cain. Caleb says in Chapter 1 that
he writes "to divert my mind from the deplorableness
of my situation," that is, as a kind of psychotherapy,
but he is certainly using his book as an antitext to the
Surprising History, which is possibly the work of Falkland himself. Autobiography here seeks to quash the

"unauthorized biography." This enactment of Giam-
battista Vico's pseudoetymologyical connection of
"author," "authority," and "owner," [8] is Caleb's desperate affirmation of freedom of soul, although in the
manuscript ending of *Caleb Williams* it shrinks until
it is the last means available to be a degenerating mind
to maintain some contact with reality.

Composition here is a double act: To write one's autobiography is to compose one's self. "In writing these
pages I obtain in the first place a means of essaying the
force of my new found understanding; and I am able,
writing as I do, uncertainly and by short snatches, to
proportion my essay to the strength of which I am conscious" (Appendix I, p.331). In this unpublished ending, Caleb's grasp on sanity slips and he slides toward
insanity, that is, towards narrative silence. His writing
is displaced by incoherent nightmares.

The published ending to the text is no less unhappy.
Having been told by Mr. Falkland's demonic minion,
Gines, that he must never, under pain of death, consider leaving the British Isles, Caleb resolves to seek justice from the law court in Mr. Falkland's home county.
This brings his physical journey and his narrative into
a circular configuration and invites the reader to think
in terms either of the wheel of fortune or the biblical
maxim that the last shall be the first. In court, Caleb
indeed triumphs: The power of his oratory is too much
even for Falkland to resist:

Williams, said he, you have conquered! I see too late
the greatness and elevation of your mind. . . . I could
have resisted any plan of malicious accusation that
you might have brought against me. But I see that the
artless and manly story you have told, has carried con-
viction to every hearer. (p. 324)

Here we are struck by the idea that the law court is a
stage, by the idea that even the most honest cause, if

pleaded by a convincing lawyer, Caleb in this case, acquires something artificial in the telling. Mr. Falkland confesses, it seems, because Caleb's rhetoric renders any defense superfluous.

The written text contains what the listening public cannot see, namely, the speaker's inner thoughts. Thus Caleb tells the truth, but, even as he reveals Falkland's crimes, he realizes his own are greater:

I began these memoirs with the idea of vindicating my character. I have now no character that I wish to vindicate: but I will finish them that thy [Falkland's] story may be fully understood; and that, if those errors of thy life be known which thou so ardently desirdst to conceal, the world may at least not hear and repeat a half-told and mangled tale. (p.326)

Caleb changes from prosecutor into attorney for the defense. One more circle closes, one more set of opposites is reconciled through synthesis. Like the theologians in Borges's story, Caleb and Falkland are, from a superhuman perspective, one and the same person.

Godwin sought to write a nonironic version of the comic indictment of romances of chivalry Cervantes wrote in *Don Quijote:* He achieved that goal, but in doing so he also produced an allegory on writing. Caleb, a better reader of romances than Falkland, reads those labyrinthine tales because they all contain a secret, a mystery—the mainspring that makes the narrative work. When his own life becomes a quest first for information and then for release from the burden entailed in possessing that information, he finds solace in writing. He has little trouble finding a genre suitable to his tale, a combination of the picaresque and the romance. The result of this blend is a confessional romance in which satire is displaced by irony: No sooner does Caleb confabulate a self through writing than he must lose that self in the discovery that the identity he so eagerly sought to preserve belongs to someone else.

At the same time, the text remains a monument to a dead self, an elegy sung by the self in its own honor. This concept of the text as alter ego or image of the narrator reappears in Mary Shelley's *Frankenstein*, where the work of art is defined as the artist's monstrous double. The nameless monster Frankenstein creates is the Romantic work of art, beautiful in inspiration yet hideous when transformed into a printed text to be read by others. Caleb's writing is his only world because his real world is turned into a prison by Mr. Falkland: The irony begins when Caleb realizes that his text also a prison, a labyrinth at whose center his own guilty conscience waits. Falkland and Caleb are doubles, but at the same time so are Caleb and his book, and each pair is linked by guilt and remorse.

Caleb Williams is much more than a literary pendant to Godwin's *Political Justice*. It simultaneously points the way to *Frankenstein*, where the antagonistic relationship between the artist and the finished work of art is turned into an allegory, and to the writings of Samuel Beckett, where the text's desire to proliferate is presented as an intention separate from the artist himself. The other vision to be derived from Godwin's text, another Romantic myth, is the one studied by Victor Brombert, the happy prison of the self where writing (and reading) may take place: "Le prisonnier de l'espace close de l'imagination déchiffre un text qui est á la fois le sien et celui des autres" (Brombert, p.20). It is the painful process that leads finally to the escape into oneself (and writing) that Virginia Woolf describes in her satire *Orlando.*

While the narrator of *Caleb Williams* is unstable, the narrator of *Orlando* is simply mysterious. The only hint at who this narrator might be comes in the form of a Cervantine parody. When don Quijote sets out on his first sally, he exclaims, imagining what the "sage" who would one day immortalize his exploits would write:

Happy times, and happy age, in which my famous exploits shall come to light, worthy to be engraved in brass, carved in marble, and drawn in picture, for a monument to all posterity! O thou sage enchanter! whoever thou art, to whose lot it shall fall to be the chronicler of this wonderful history, I beseech thee not to forget my good Rozinante, the inseparable companion of all my travels and excursions.[9]

In subtle variation on this parody, Woolf's narrator announces:

Happy the mother who bears, happier still the biographer who records the life of such a one! Never need she vex herself, nor he invoke the help of novelist or poet. From deed to deed, from glory to glory, from office to office he must go, his scribe following after, till they reach whatever seat it may be that is the height of their desire.[10]

The juxtaposition of mother and biographer in this passage links the beginning of *Orlando* to its conclusion, where Orlando gives birth simultaneously to a book and a child. About the child the reader learns nothing; the published text, "The Oak Tree," marks the moment when Orlando finally achieves the status of writer, which had eluded her for several centuries. The reader knows very little about "The Oak Tree" beyond its title and the fact that Orlando works on it steadily from Elizabethan times until its publication. Like Caleb Williams's picaresque narratives, it is enclosed, metaphorically, within another book, the anonymous biography we are reading. Quijote, in the passage quoted above, addresses an imaginary "sage enchanter" who will write his history in the style of the romances. Cervantes, in a burst of self-reflecting irony, mocks himself as Quijote's bard and then proceeds to bombard the reader with every sort of displaced authorial presence: This is a found manuscript, an incomplete text, and a translation from the Arabic by a Moor (a people known to be unreliable). Above all, the *Quijote*, because of Cervantes's use of these Renaissance author-text tricks, is an anonymous book.

This anonymity links Cervantes to Woolf. As Maria di Battista succinctly puts it:

The creative power of women differed, Woolf felt, from the creative power of men, but she insisted that the success and expression of that power depended on that impersonality or anonymity, that absence of special pleading, which lends to art "that curious quality which comes only when sex is unconscious of itself."[11]

The anonymity of Orlando's biographer is, then, a mask. The author of the biography and the author of "The Oak Tree" are one and the same.

A similar Cervantine trickery animates Nabokov's *The Real Life of Sebastian Knight*, where the writer's half-brother seeks information about the deceased Sebastian Knight only to find more enigmas at every turn. In the last chapter, the reader suspects that the true author of the novel is Sebastian Knight and that any attempt by a writer at autobiography inevitably ends in biography, in the creation of a chracter. The writer's destiny is anonymity, the moment when he ceases to be a personality and becomes a text—the creation that justifies his existence as a name. The ambition that leads a person to seek immortality through writing ends in disillusion when the writer discovers that it is not he who has survived but language. This is the lesson of the entire career of Jorge Luis Borges, translator of *Orlando* into Spanish.

We see here two attitudes toward writing: In Godwin writing is a means to maintain at least the illusion of individual identity, even though Caleb Williams's first-person narrative leads fatally to despair and madness. This is the central problem of the first-person mode: How do they end? Cervantes himself explores the problem in the famous galley-slave incident in *Don Quijote*, part 1, chapter 22 [12]. Despite the threat of annihilation that hangs over the first-person narrator who stops writing, this form of narration is a consolation to the fugitive or to the prisoner whose only liberty is within himself.

The other attitude is the one we find in Virginia Woolf, the one expounded by Reinaldo Arenas, namely, an attitude that deflects the act of writing away from the ego and projects it into masks and anonymity. It is tempting to compare Cervantes and Woolf with the authors of the picaresque tradition, in fact with all writers of first-person narratives. The first-person is best suited for didactic (and, naturally, mock-didactic) purposes: The reader sees the world from a single, albeit often bizarre or mad point of view, and learns about the inner turmoil of an often pathetic individual with whom he may easily identify. The third-person narrative, despite the appearance of the so-called omniscient narrator in so many nineteenth-century novels, allows for more ambiguity (more points of view) and certainly for no less irony.

The ideal compromise between these narrative paradigms is the epistolary form popularized by Richardson and raised to perfection by Laclos. The epistolary novel has all but disappeared in the twentieth century and has been replaced by another form in which the narrative moves back and forth from first to third person as it suits the needs of the author. This is the result of the development of the psychological novel from Flaubert to James, Proust, and Joyce, and of the revolution against narrative decorum that took place during

the early decades of this century among various avant-
garde groups, particularly the Surrealists.

We see the Spanish American version of that tradition in Reinaldo Arenas's *El mundo alucinante*, a self-
conscious rewriting of an extant text in which the first-
person structure is shattered so that a Surrealist liberation of imagination may take place. The notion of rewriting, which entails parody, also involves the
concept of appropriation. Arenas makes someone else's
writing his own by translating it into his own idiom.
He accomplishes what usually occurs in reading or interpretation, namely, the production of a new text,
much in the way the narrator of Borges's story "Pierre
Menard, Author of the *Quijote*," finds Pierre Menard's
version of Cervantes's text richer than the original
even though the two are textually identical. *El mundo
alucinante* enacts an allegory of reading, one that eras-
es differences between reader and text in order to turn
the text into a mirror.

Arenas's narrator begins by "turning his back on his
public" and addressing his subject, Fray Servando
Teresa de Mier (1763-1827), whose *Memoirs* (1876) he
rewrites. The effect of this apostrophe, which appears
here as a letter, is paradoxical: On the one hand it invokes the spirit of the long-absent Fray Servando, but
on the other it holds Fray Servando off at a distance.
Paul Fry's remarks on the peculiar relationship between apostrophe and dialectic in odes clarify what
happens in Arenas's address to Fray Servando:

If dialectic in the ode is a turning back upon or
against the self, according to Socrates' understanding
of dialectic as an "interrupting question," apostrophe,
the blanket form of *invocatio*, is defined in all the
Rhetorics as a turning aside to address some absent
hearer. Hence dialectic, the figure of thought (which
subverts *itself*), and apostrophe, the figure of speech,

subvert each other, and the poet confirms his solitude
by crying out for company. In fact, though, apostrophe
in general does not call for the presence of the ad-
dressee. . . . The poet speaks these asides to a pro tem
audience and then returns to the audience that is understood to be listening, as it were, under contract.
(*Poet's Calling*, p.11)

While it pretends to call attention to another (Fray Servando), Arenas's apostrophe calls attention to itself as
Arenas's utterance. The apostrophe is an act of self-affirmation, as Jonathan Culler calls it, "a figure of vocation,"[13] whereby the speaker identifies himself as an
artist. Apostrophe as a device to announce that one is
an artist characterizes the rest of Arenas's epistle: He
describes how he first came upon Fray Servando in a
miserable history of Mexican literature, how he unsuc-
cessfully sought information about him in libraries,
museums, and embassies, how his quest was frustrated
until he made what he calls a "useful" discovery: "The
most useful thing was to discover that you and I are the
same person" (p.9). This discovery changed the nature
of their relationship:

De aquí que toda referencia anterior hasta llegar a este
descubrimiento formidable e insoportable sea in-
necesaria y casi la he desechado por completo. Sólo
tus memorias . . . aparecen en este libro, no como
citas de un texto extraño, sino como parte fundamental del mismo, donde resulta innecesario recalcar que
son tuyas; porque no es verdad, porque son, en fin,
como todo lo grandioso y grotesco, del tiempo. (So
that any earlier references, prior to this formidable
and unbearable discovery are unnecessary. I've prac-
tically rejected all of them. Only your memoirs . . .
appear in this book, not as quotations from someone
else's text but as a fundamental part of this one. It is
therefore unnecessary to repeat that they belong to

you: Because it isn't true, because, like everything
grand and grotesque, they belong to time.) (pp.9-10)

Arenas's letter to Fray Servando, as strong an example
of invocation used as a sign of literary vocation as any
apostrophe in a lyric, leaves the reader perplexed: First
Fray Servando is the object of an investigation, then he
is taken to be identical to the person seeking him out,
and finally he becomes anonymous, an incident in
time, a text. The image of Pierre menard again comes
to mind: When Pierre Menard thinks about writing
(not rewriting), he has an image of Cervantes's novel in
his memory that corresponds to the dim vision any
novelist has of an as yet unwritten novel.

In a similar way, Arenas writes a novel whose protagonist is Fray Servando and incorporates into his test
quotations from the autobiographical writings of Fray
Servando. Arenas identifies himself with the Mexican
monk, but how? As another politically persecuted individual? As someone like Caleb Williams whose only
life is writing? This last possibility is germane to *El
mundo alucinante:* Arenas, like Fray Servando, found
that writing was his ultimate reason for being. But the
same difference exists between Arenas's narrative and
Fray Servando's as exists between Godwin's and
Woolf's: Godwin and Fray Servando are ultimately
concerned with the conservation of individual ego—
the first-person narrator—while Woolf and Arenas are
concerned with the act of literary creation. Woolf and
Arenas realize that the first-person or, in Arenas's case,
the use of all possible narrators, gives the writer max-
imum freedom.

In Woolf and Arenas the quest for freedom of expression or freedom from persecution does not trace
the pathetic vicissitudes of a single individual but
turns toward the generation of a text whose true subject is writing itself. This is a secondary theme in *Cal-*

eb Williams and Fray Servando's memoirs, but it is present in both, in Caleb's constant turn to writing both as a source of income and as a means of pleading his case before posterity, and in Fray Servando's constant scribbling, his only means of attacking enemies and presenting himself as a bizarre species of martyr.

The notion, strong in Western literature since Romanticism, that even if the body is imprisoned the soul or imagination remains free is the thread that connects Godwin, Fray Servando, and Woolf. It is also true that in all three the idea of the prison expands from the individual cell to include the whole world as a scene of persecution. Whenever Caleb tries to escape from Falkland he finds someone tracking him down; at the end he realizes he can never escape from his own guilt. Even after Fray Servando escapes from the Inquisition, he finds others in his native Mexico ready to imprison him.

Woolf breaks with this model of endless persecution. Orlando discovers in 1928, the year *Orlando* is published, that she has finally reached a point in history where she is free to be herself. Even if his text is shaped by *Orlando*, Arenas does not place liberation in a historical context. In fact, his book—radically different in this sense from *Orlando*—negates the very idea of progress. This is clear from his statement in the prefatory letter about being one and the same person with Fray Servando. Both the writer (Fray Servando) and the rewriter (Arenas) must discover their own literary freedom within the limits of bondage.

Arenas has one recourse Fray Servando does not have: the literature of the avant-garde, especially Surrealism, which proposed to liberate the imagination of both artists and their public. In a way, *El mundo alucinante* is an aesthetic elaboration of Borges's essay "Kafka and his Precursors," where we read:

The poem "Fears and Scruples" by Robert Browning prophecies the writing of Kafka, but our reading of Kafka sharpens and detours out reading of the poem a good deal. Browning did not read as we now read him. In critical discourse the word *precursor* is indispensable, but we should make an effort to purify it of all connotations of polemics or rivalries. The fact is that each writer *creates* his precursors. His work modifies our concept of the past, just as it will modify the future.[14]

Just as each reader recreates the text by reading it, turning it into a version of his own experience, the reader also recreates literary history, making connections— Borges's precursors—unimagined by the author. Arenas rewrites Fray Servando: His pretext is that he and Fray Servando are one. Yet what we actually see here is Fray Servando's book turned into a mirror, a "hallucinated world" more akin to Kafka than to the late eighteenth century. Looking further back in time we find William Godwin, who we inevitable read as a precursor of both Kafka and Arenas.

These affinities in no way deprive the texts of individual value; they simply trace their fate once in the hands of readers. To read *El mundo alucinante,* for example, it is not necessary to have read Fray Servando's memoirs. Everything in Fray Servando suffers a seachange in Arenas's rewriting, to the point that the book constantly taunts the reader by offering, then taking away narrative possibilities:

Venimos del corojal. No venimos del corojal. Yo y las dos Josefas venimos del corojal. Vengo solo del corojal y ya casi se está haciendo de noche. (We're coming from the palm grove. We aren't coming from the palm grove. The two Josefas and I are coming from the palm grove. I'm coming from the palm grove by myself and it's almost getting dark.) (p.11)

The entire text is a constantly shifting structure in which what is narrated in one chapter, even one sentence, is negated in the next. This tactic is intended to frustrate the reader seeking a story and either to repel him or to make him into what Julio Cortázar, in *Hopscotch*, calls an "accomplice reader." The purpose of all this is to liberate the reader from misconceptions about literature—its purpose is not necessarily to amuse or edify the reader—and about reading—it is an active, not a passive, operation. For Arenas, as for Woolf, the creation of the literary text is a function of a human need for aesthetic expression, but the "content" of that expression is always subordinated to the act of expression itself.

The act of writing in *El mundo alucinante*, as in some of Samuel Beckett's writings, is not a matter of pleasure but of necessity. It is a habit which, once begun, can never be broken. Arenas describes Fray Servando's "fall" into writing early in *El mundo alucinante*, when he describes, in the third person, Fray Servando mentally parodying an epigram by Martial. Then, in the second person, addressing Fray Servando (or himself) directly, he says:

De modo que caíste en el veneno de la literatura y revolviste polillas y papeles sin encontrar nada. Y todo no fue más que una suma de interrogantes no contestados que agitaron más tus inquietudes ya habituales. Y quisiste saber. Y preguntaste. Y seguite investigando sin que nadie te pudiera decir nada, sino que dejaras esas lecturas que mucho tenían de sacrilegio y de locura.(And so you fell into the poison of literature and you meddled in dust and papers without finding anything. And all of it was nothing more than a mass of unanswered questions that whipped up your already habitual uncertainties even more. And you wanted to know. And you asked. And you went on investigating without anyone's being able to say a word to you, except that you should desist from those readings that had much of sacrilege and madness to them.) (p.29)

The birth of the writer occurs in three distinct phases: He seeks (for what, it cannot be said), he reads, and he parodies the works of other writers. At the same time, the narrator describes these activities as dangerous, because they may entail heresy or lead to madness. They are also necessarily clandestine: Fray Servando must read contraband books, among them *Don Quijote*, which alarms some customs officials. The writer, in the best Romantic tradition, is considered suspicious by a society that regards all writing as potentially subversive.

Thus Fray Servando becomes the archetypal persecuted artist, a specific category of the fugitive—Caleb Williams. Unlike Caleb, Fray Servando does not become an artist to make a living: He is more like Orlando in that his life is art waiting for an artist to make aesthetic use of it. Woolf creates an archetypal female writer, who is in many ways herself, and writes a life for that character in the form of a biography. Arenas finds his double in history and makes him into a character by rewriting his autobiographical texts.

When Arenas depicts his alter ego in jail, imprisoned for having delivered a heretical sermon on the miraculous appearance of the Virgin of Guadalupe in Mexico, he quite naturally shows him as a Romantic prisoner-artist longing to write. Although Fray Servando is dying of thirst, his thirst for writing is greater than his physical need. What he longs to redact are his ideas, even if, as he admits to himself, writing is ultimately unsatisfactory:

Y sin embargo, pensó, mientras gritaba por agua y por luz, como un nuevo y reciente mito, las mejores ideas

son precisamente las que nunca logro llevar al papel,
porque dicho hecho ya les hace perder la magia de lo
imaginado y porque el resquicio del pensamiento en
que se alojan no permite que sean escudriñadas, y al
sacarlas de ali, salen trastocadas, cambiadas y de-
formes. (And yet, he thought, as he shouted for water
and light, like a new and recent myth, the best ideas
are those I never succeed in getting down on paper,
because the very act makes them lose the magic of
the imaginary and because the narrow space of the
thought in which they are lodged does not allow them
to be scrutinized; when they are taken out, they
emerge twisted around, changed, and deformed.) (p.44)

This is Arenas's version of what transpires in *Frankenstein*. In that semi-epistolary novel, Mary Shelley creates, echoing Shelley's "Alastor," a frustrated Romantic artist who creates, in a parody of divine creation and
human procreation, something immortal and hideous.
The nameless monster is an object of loathing to his
creator precisely because as an idea he is beautiful and
becomes ugly only when "published," released from
Frankenstein's imagination into the world. Public language, in the Romantic view, is inadequate to represent the inspirations of the artist: The result is that the
work of art is always the faulty reconstruction of an
inexpressible mental work of art. These ideas may help
to explain why Arenas's narrative so often works
against itself by proposing and then rejecting narrative
possibilities and why the text is so amorphous, moving
from episode to episode with no apparent pattern.

An example of this formlessness appears in chapter
14, "Concerning the Friar's Visit to the Gardens of the
King." In this first-person sequence, Fray Servando describes a Kafkaesque search for the king of Spain,
whose gardens are patterned on Bosch's "Garden of
Earthly Delights." Naturally, these scenes have nothing to do with Fray Servando's memoirs, but they are

central to Arenas's vision of Fray Servando as artist. Searching for the king, Fray Servando finds a young man who offers to guide him. This guide saves Fray Servando, first from a group of suicidal women, and later from a boiling stream: Fray Servando tries to dive into this stream after diving into an ice-cold stream, although why he jumps into either stream he does not say. The cold bath seems to be a prelude because the boy announces to Fray Servando that he is about to enter the "tres tierras del amor" (three lands of love) (p.88). Fray Servando finds all three disagreeable because none gives happiness, the very existence of which he doubts.

The boy suggests that Fray Servando's doubts about the existence of happiness explain why he cannot join any of the three groups of love, but that "hay un grupo que no tiene trascendencia, y en el cual podrías encontrarte *tú contigo.*" (there is a group that lacks transcendence and in which you may find you yourself) (p.91). This is the zone of the "desperdicios" (rejects), those who constitute the waste of the other categories. There Fray Servando finds a man writing. He accidentally interrupts the man, who instantly hangs himself. The guide informs Fray Servando that the writer was composing his masterpiece and that being interrupted caused him to commit suicide. Fray Servando feels horribly guilty, but his guide calms him, saying, "No te preocupes, que ese hombre jamás hubiera terminado su obra, no olvides que está as en *la tierra de los que buscan,* y por lo tanto, nada encontrarán." (Don't worry, that man never would have finished, don't forget that you're in the land of those who seek, and who, for that reason, find nothing) (p.92). Concerned about the fate of the masterpiece, Fray Servando is informed that precisely because it is a masterpiece it can never be finished. The journey comes to an end, and Fray Servando expresses his disappointment at not having seen the king, whereupon the guide announces he is the king and that the freedom Fray Servando seeks is absurd: "¿Para qué quieres modificar lo que precisamente te forma?" (Why do you want to change exactly that thing that forms you?) (p.95). That is, what Fray Servando wants is to cease to be himself, in effect, to lose his identity, an idea the king defines as a horror worse than either the fruitless quest or prison itself.

The dialogue breaks off and the reader is left in mystery, until chapter 27, when Fray Servando visits England. There he meets Virginia Woolf's Orlando, who acts as his guide, thereby serving as a parallel to the mysterious king of chapter 14. Orlando describes her metamorphosis to Fray Servando, adding: "Mi vida no ha sido más que una constante búsqueda, sin ningún acierto." (My life has been nothing more than a constant quest, with no discovery) (p.159). This reiteration of the quest (*búsqueda*) motif links Arenas's Fray Servando to Orlando: Both are projections of the artist and both are condemned to seek, that is, to write. This sentence modifies, as Brombert notes, the idea of the Romantic prison, transforming the act of writing into imprisonment, turning the production of texts into a jail sentence. The idea of the unfinished masterpiece here is an ironic echo of Balzac's *Le Chef-d'oeuvre Inconnu*. In that novel, Balzac criticizes the Romantic mystique of the "incommunicable vision,"[15] demanding that the personal, idiosyncratic vision be subordinated to the precepts of art.

This subordination is the cornerstone of the Realist novel and marks the point of divergence between lyric poetry and prose narrative in the nineteenth century. Twentieth-century artists seem less willing to sacrifice their obsessions to communication, less able to accommodate their vision to a language accessible to the "common reader." If there is a crisis in literary production in the second half of the twentieth century, it results from the writer's simultaneous need to express himself and a desire to communicate his vision to readers. There are no simple answers to this problem, and texts like *El mundo alucinante* dramatize it by oscillating between realism and idiosyncratic self-expression.

This dilemma, however, is not one all writers have the luxury to deal with as they please, especially writers who live in societies that demand adherence to a specific aesthetic. Important in this connection is another "real person" Fray Servando meets in London: José Blanco White. The real Fray Servando did have contact with Blanco White, a Spanish liberal exiled in England, and published two important letters about the revolt of Spain's American colonies in Blanco's magazine. But Blanco is important for Arenas for the same reason he has been important for Spanish intellectuals and artists since the Spanish Civil War: He typifies the writer in exile, the Spaniard who attempts to translate himself into an Englishmen, risking madness in the process.

Thus it is that in the latter part of *El mundo alucinante* references to Cuban writers in exile in genuine exile or, as in the case of José Lezama Lima, in a state of ostracism) proliferate. Areans makes Fray Servando's companion in Mexico the Cuban Romantic poet José María de Heredia, who dies in Mexico. The two have nothing in common, do not understand each other, and yet live together because they are both condemned to be perpetually out of place—strangers at home or abroad. There is a reference in chapter 28 to a certain "habanero Infante" thrown overboard by the sailors bringing Fray Servando back to Mexico. This unknown figure is aboard "as a man of letters and journalist" (p. 173) and infuriates the sailors by writing a sonnet to the sea during a storm. The reference to Guillermo Cabrera Infante is vague but clear enough, just as references to "José Lezamis" (p. 201) and "the jailing of Padilla" (p. 218) are sufficient to remind us of the fate of these modern Cuban writers, José Lezama Lima and Heberto Padilla.

In this way, Arenas, as he closes the circle of his narrative by bringing Fray Servando back to Mexico, brings the reader back to the twentieth century and to the situation of a Cuban writer who finds himself incarcerated in a land where the free exercise of the imagination is as dangerous an activity as Fray Servando's sermon on the Virgin of Guadalupe. The persecution and imprisonment that begin in Godwin as social persecution and end there with the production of a text, the imprisonment of the female imagination that ends in Woolf in a twentieth century willing to accept the idea of a female writer, returns in Arenas to haunt the reader.

The double imprisonment of the writer who finds himself in a society hostile to the liberated imagination is a real factor for a writer such as Arenas, who has had to leave Cuba and become yet one more writer in exile. Threats to the artist my be metaphoric, imaginary, real, or, in historic terms "the fate of the artist since Romanticism," but for Arenas time in many societies seems to have stopped. For every free Orlando there remain many in jail or exile. *El mundo alucinante* is a hallucinatory vision of a world that cannot exist. Unfortunately is does: It is our world.

4

Lewis Carroll and Jorge Luis Borges:
Mock Epic as Autobiography

Despite the exertions of Robert Southey, Milton seems to have laid the epic to rest. Hegel, Lukács, and their followers have associated this event in literary history with the history of culture, with what they see as its decline during the so-called bourgeois era, and have designated the novel as the epic's decadent avatar in the modern age. These critics of the novel always qualify the parallel by including strictures about the "prosaic" (Hegel)[1] world the novel seeks to represent or about the novel's incomplete and therefore inferior representation of reality (Lukács).[2] For Lukács the reality the novel seeks to represent is fragmented; therefore, the genre's frantic attempt to forge (in all senses of the word) a total vision of it is doomed beforehand to failure.

Why is it axiomatic that the novel should correspond in modern times to what the epic was in that nebulous age Hegel and Lukács call the "classical period"? Their meditations on literature—it would be unfair to call them serious theories of literary genres—attempt to relate literature to a history of culture which for them has both a direction and a clear meaning. And to ensure conformity between literature and history they sacrifice precision on the literary side in order to have that symmetry in the flow of history. The ideological imperative of a Lukács is clear and rather distressing: He obviously loves the novel but must define it as the failed epic of the failing bourgeois era.

The literary lesson to be derived from both Hegel and Lukács with regard to the novel—to what makes the novel different from the other narrative forms—is its tendency toward the encyclopedic, which has been true since Cervantes published the second part of the *Quijote* in 1615. The *Quijote* is not merely the "origin," the source of the novel as we know it, but an encyclopedia of narrative forms—those Cervantes and contemporary critics recognized. It is also a mock-epic of encylopedic tendency, a compendium of what could be called secular myths, stories about ordinary people functioning within the structure of ordinary society. This is precisely the point of don Quijote's madness: Illusion and delusion are the only things that can make an ordinary individual interesting or meaningful. Cervantes resolves the quandary of how to make normal life into literary material by means of a protagonist who thinks he is extraordinary.

Cervantine madness generates a whole body of literature, one that consciously blends myths derived not only from secular literature (the romances Cervantes explicitly parodies in the *Quijote*) but from sacred literature as well: That Quijote is a mock or parodic Christ is an idea Cervantes's contemporaries may either have prudently overlooked or simply understood as an aspect of the work's carnivalesque nature, but it is certainly a notion Dostoevsky took very seriously. And it is that deliberate (mis)appropriation of sacred mythology a critic like Lukács refuses to see.

From Boccaccio to Cervantes to Dostoevsky, authors of narrative have turned to the Bible (and to other kinds of sacred writing, such as saints' lives) for stories they retell in parodic or pathetic form. Where Lukács sees a failure in the novel to recreate bourgeois life in its totality, a more charitable reader might see the novel as the literary genre that gathers together all of mankind's myths precisely to demonstrate the differences between sacred and demotic writing. Northrop Frye defines the Bible as "a gigantic myth, a narrative extending over the whole of time from creation to apocalypse, unified by a body of recurring imagery that "freezes" into a single metaphor cluster, the metaphors all being identified with the body of the Messiah, the man who is all men, the totality of *logoi* who is one Logos, the grain of sand that is the world."[3] Frye goes on to point out that it is language that links the Bible and secular literature:

The *kerygma*, or proclaiming rhetoric, of the Bible is a welcoming and approaching rhetoric, addressed by a male God to a symbolically female body of readers. Coming the other way is the body of human imaginative response, as we have it in literature and the arts, where the language is purely imaginative and hence hypothetical. Here the imaginative product seems to be symbolically female, the daughter of a Muse. Yet perhaps it is only through the study of works of human imagination that we can make any real contact with the level of vision beyond faith. For such vision is, among other things, the quality in all serious religions that enables them to be associated with human products of culture and imagination, where the limit is the conceivable and not the actual. (*Great Code*, pp.231–32)

Where the Bible subordinates all stories to one story, secular literature seeks diversity—which explains why we must read these two kinds of writing in different ways—even when secular literature—the texts of Dante, Cervantes, or Joyce—seems to strive for some organic unity. Nevertheless, secular narratives, perhaps by their very nature, never achieve the total unity Frye ascribes to biblical narrative. This may be why secular narrative so often alludes to its own limitations through the medium of parody. Frye suggests this in the *Anatomy of Criticism*:

The theme of encylopaedic parody is endemic in satire, and in prose fiction is chiefly to be found in the anatomy, the tradition of Apuleius and Rabelais and Swift. Satires and novels show a relation corresponding to that of epics and narratives: the more novels a novelist writes the more successful he is, but Rabelais, Burton, and Sterne build their creative lives around one supreme effort. Hence it is in satire and irony that we should expect that the containing form of the ironic or satiric epic would be the pure cycle, in which every quest, however successful or heroic, has sooner or later to be made over again. (p.321)

Frye creates a ratio or proportion: Satires are to novels as epics are to narratives, suggesting that while a culture may have only one central epic, that epic gives rise to or sanctions the existence of an entire field of stories. Satires, he adds, are analogous to epics in that they seek to take in all possible satiric themes. The novel, like nonepic narrative, conquers by sheer force of numbers, which may explain why the novel, in all its permutations, rapidly becomes, after Cervantes, the standard form of narrative. By novel we understand an extended fiction of a more or less realistic sort with psychologically true-to-life characters who change and develop in an environment whose parameters are set by those of the real world, which in turn is organized according to linear, progressive historiographic principles. Obviously, a global definition of the novel, one that would encompass the worlds of both Stendhal and Trollope is of necessity vague or even impossible given the peculiar flexibility of the genre, but some limited definition must be set in order to distinguish the novel from other narrative types. What Hegel and Lukács teach us is that if we really want to understand the history of narrative types we must look beyond simplistic reductions.

Mock-epic is an ideal case in point. If we believe Aristotle, mock-epic is as old as epic itself:

However, just as on the serious side Homer was most truly a poet, since he was the only one who not only composed well but constructed dramatic imitations, so too he was the first to adumbrate the forms of comedy by producing a (1) dramatic presentation, and not of invective but of (2) the ludicrous. For as the *Iliad* stands in relation to our tragedies, so the *Margites* stands in relation to our comedies.[4]

It is certainly one of the principal perversities of literary history that Aristotle's remarks on the *Margites* have survived while not a single verse of the actual poem has reached us. Nonetheless, mock epic, a species of satire—Aristotle carefully separates it from satiric invective[5]—has been a constant in Western literature since the Renaissance.

Even if few twentieth-century texts are overtly mock-epics, the form still makes itself felt. Since the eighteenth century, it has undergone several metamorphoses and appears most often now as the mock epyllion, the short epic in verse or prose. Thus it blends into the larger body of satiric writing, its prose manifestations fusing with the vague literary corpus we call the short story. What we find in these texts is exactly the opposite of the encyclopedic tendency of novelistic writing. Frye notes that encyclopedic forms serve as gathering places for conventional themes—the various inn scenes in the *Quijote* dramatize this tendency of the encylopedic text to provide a setting in which stories meet and intertwine—and that these themes become episodes in the larger text. He adds:

The reverse development occurs when a lyric on a conventional theme achieves a concentration that expands it into a miniature epic: if not the historical "little epic" or epyllion, something very like it generically. Thus *Lycidas* is a miniature scriptural epic extending over the whole range covered by *Paradise Lost*, the death of man and his redemption by Christ.... In modern times the miniature epic becomes a very common form: the later poems of Eliot, of Edith Sitwell, and many cantos of Pound belong to it. (*Anatomy*, p.324)

Lewis Carroll's *The Hunting of the Snark* (1876)[6] and Jorge Luis Borges's short story "Tlön, Uqbar, Orbis Tertius" (1940)[7] exemplify this concentration of energy in a small space. Both texts combine specific strains of mock epic—the mock wisdom epic and the mock quest epic—with very personal autobiographical allegories about the artist's loss of identity in a life given over to the manipulation of language.

Writing on Milton's epics, James C. Nohrnberg depicts the relationship between the various types of epic writing by means of the diagram in figure 1.

Nohrnberg explains the rationalê for his diagram in this way:

All epics have a vertical aspect in the descent of heaven. If there exists an equally universal horizontal aspect, it must be the wars of migration or ascendancy of the divine establishment, and the migration of peoples when this divine establishment fails or removes to a further domain. From these two themes come the two major concepts with which an epic works, namely territoriality and reconnaissance. The territory may be authoritatively secured—occupied by divine right—or violently disputed; the reconnaissance may be aggressively pursued, or it may be an act of unmoved contemplation. From these four combinations emerge four possible epics: the "creation" or foundation epic, the strife epic, the quest epic, and the "survey" or wisdom epic.[8]

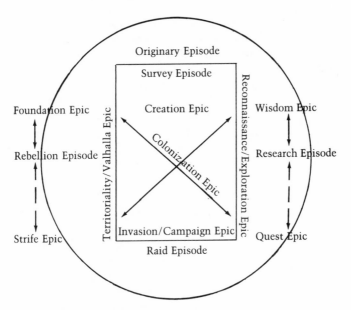

Figure 1. The Types of Epics

Nohrnberg associates the quest epic with the god Hermes and "the tantalizing or Hesperidean apple of inordinate desire" which reminds us that the "serious" quest epic already contained in it elements of picaresque humor, that Odysseus is both a hero and a *pícaro*. What Nohrnberg demonstrates, a matter that again differentiates between the encyclopedic and the "simple" forms, is that genuine epic writing includes all of the different epic types, that there is a will-to-totality in epic writing, one appropriately represented by Professor Nohrnberg's circle.

This is not the case with mock epic, especially as Lewis Carroll and Borges manipulate it, although as Nohrnberg observes, "The conclusion of a mock-quest epic like *The Hunting of the Snark*, for example, displaces the announced adventure into a quizzical research episode." That is, as one story ends, it announces the beginning of another. This continuity is not actually present in either *The Snark* or "Tlön," which both have eschatological endings. The truncated, fragmentary aspect of both texts marks them as products of the post-Romantic era: The zeal any modern writer shows when attempting the all-embracing encyclopedic text; *Finnegans Wake* for instance, is mocked beforehand by the futile gropings of Flaubert's late-blooming encyclopedists Bouvard and Pecuchet.

The amount of knowledge any single author can possess is limited, as is his ability to translate knowledge into a literary text: The gap between what he expresses and what he is capable of expressing becomes an abyss. To avoid despair, the modern writer necessarily deludes himself, especially with regard to self-expression. Eventually doubts about the existence of the self creep in, and the author realizes that his function as an artist is to reprocess language. The longer he works at his craft the fainter his hopes for originality become. Humpty-Dumpty's boast about being the master of language in *Through the Looking-Glass*[9] is an ironic parody of the modern writer's relationship with language: Language ultimately absorbs him until, like the Baker in *The Snark*, he "softly and suddenly" vanishes away.

Why would Lewis Carroll think a mock quest epic based on a hunt would be the appropriate vehicle for a story of pathetic failure? There can be no absolute answer to this, and Carroll's persistent declarations of ignorance about the poem's meaning confirm its ultimate ambiguity. The following sequence suggests a possible transition from *Through the Looking-Glass* to *The Snark*: Life in looking-glass world is arranged like a huge game of chess. Alice suddenly understands the meaning of the game and just as suddenly conceives an ambition:

"I declare it's marked out just like a large chessboard!" Alice said at last. "There ought to be men moving about somewhere—and so there are!" she added in a tone of delight, and her heart began to beat quick with excitement as she went on. "It's a great huge game of chess that's being played—all over the world—if this *is* the world at all, you know. Oh, what fun it is! How I *wish* I was one of them! I wouldn't mind being a Pawn, if only I might join— though of course I should *like* to be a Queen, best." (*Annotated Alice*, pp.207-8)

The Alice books are extraterritorial adventure tales linked thematically to the raid episode in Nohrnberg's diagram. In this looking-glass-world passage, inspired perhaps by the son's Siegfried-like slaying of the Jabberwock in the mock-Anglo-Saxon poem of chapter 1, Alice passes from observer to participant. That is, her adventure-foray becomes a genuine strife epyllion— the war for which the game of chess is metaphor. Alice, like Eve in *Paradise Lost*, is seduced by a desire to be more than she is. She will become a queen but only by sacrificing her childhood: To play the game of life the child must "fall" into adulthood, become "impure," and, ultimately, die.

Chess is a game; life here is a huge chess game. But a huge game is also a big game, and big game is something Victorian English hunters had to take sea voyages to find. "Chess" through the magic of punning evokes the "chase." *The Snark* is a big-game hunt that combines the game of life with a tragic version of the son's triumph over the Jabberwock. Alice plays her part, assuming she will become a queen and be greater than she is; similarly, the hunters in *The Snark* who accompany the Bellman are also trying to become more than they are.

This desire for increase played out on a sea adventure evokes Ulysses, both in Dante and in Tennyson. Contemporary readers saw the similarity between Tennyson and Henry Holiday's depiction of Carroll's Bellman, and it is not impossible that *The Snark* contains some parodic allusions to Tennyson, whose poems Carroll had parodied as early as 1856. Tennyson's "Ulysses" is a high-flown speech by Odysseus as he prepares to set sail in old age for his last adventure. Tennyson exalts the idea of Odysseus's sailing out to meet death in a final adventure rather than passively waiting for death at home. Tennyson contradicts Dante, who condemns Ulysses for using his rhetorical powers perversely and convincing his companions to sail beyond the limits of human experience. But this sea-voyage *topos*, either an exaltation of the human spirit or a confirmation of human limitations, is a secondary theme in *The Snark*, which is actually a hunting poem whose drama takes place on the island of the Snark.

Carroll parodies the big-game hunt, something he had already ridiculed on the level of myth (dragon-slaying) in "Jabberwocky." Carroll explicitly relates *The Snark* and "Jabberwocky" in the preface to *The Snark*, saying "this poem is to some extent connected with the lay of the Jabberwock" (*The Snark*, p.34). The two poems also have the same abab rhyme scheme. The first stanza of "Jabberwocky," the one Humpty-Dumpty "explains" to Alice, describes an evening ("brillig") scene in nature, with burrowing badgers ("toves") that upset parrots ("borogoves") and turtles ("raths"). A father cautions his son about three beasts: the Jabberwock, the Jubjub bird, and the Bandersnatch. The son enters the forest (the "tulgey wood"), meets a Jabberwock, cuts off its head, and brings the trophy back to his joyful father. In *The Snark* there is no Jabberwock, although one of the crewmen, the Butcher, identifies the shriek of the Jubjub bird and another, the Banker, is attacked by the Bandersnatch. The attack is unsuccessful, but the Banker is so terrified that he goes mad: He turns black in the face, chants incoherently, and rattles the kind of bones (a species of castanet) that the Mister Bones character in vaudeville would shake in counterpoint to Mister Tambo's tambourine.

Carroll wrote "Jabberwocky" in mock-Anglo-Saxon, which he created to amuse his brothers and sisters in a family magazine, *Misch-Masch*, in 1855. Carroll printed the first stanza of "Jabberwocky," in pseudo-Gothic script and entitled it "Stanza of Anglo-Saxon Poetry." If *The Snark* is an extrapolation and parody of what already is a parody, we have a text that shifts its parody of the hunt from language (mock-Anglo-Saxon) to the relationship between language and thought, language taken not as a form of speech but as the code out of which the author carves his text. The humor of "Jabberwocky" derives from our attempts to make sense of nonsense, as Alice herself says: "Somehow it seems to fill my head with ideas—only I don't know exactly what they are! However, *somebody* killed *something*: that's clear, at any rate" (*Annotated Alice*, p.197). *The Snark*'s humor is different: Even though it includes some nonsense language (much of it taken directly from *Through the Looking-Glass*), it, like the Alice books, generates its humor from comic characters.

The Snark is the parodic culmination of Lewis Carroll's lifelong fascination with heroic literature: It begins with the "Stanza of Anglo-Saxon Poetry" of 1855 and continues in *Through the Looking-Glass* with the chess board, "Jabberwocky," the White Knight, and the conflict between the Lion and the Unicorn. Even the battle between Tweedledum and Tweedledee has heroic dimensions: It alludes to the tale of the battling twins Balin and Balan in Malory. Nevertheless, the central theme in *The Snark* is the hunt, the foray into nature in search of big, potentially dangerous game. This raid into nature is comparable to Alice's decision to join the chess game in *Through the Looking-Glass*: The gratuitous raid (the hunt or Alice's intrusion into the looking-glass world) becomes a struggle for survival.

The fall into sexual maturity in *Through the Looking-Glass* is the price Alice pays for playing, so her winning entails a loss—which is why her triumphal banquet is so disappointing. In *The Snark*, the game being played is life itself, and since the adversary is death, losing, for Carroll, is inevitable. Alice and the Bellmans's crew succumb to temptation and become, so to speak, professional players. Thus, following Nohrnberg's diagram of the epic process, they move from Quest through Raid to Temptation and on towards Wisdom. In both texts gain is balanced by loss: This is suggested in *Through the Looking-Glass* when the flowers hint that Alice is growing old, when Humpty-Dumpty wonders why she doesn't stop counting her birthdays at seven, and when the scented rushes Alice picks while punting with the Sheep immediately lose their perfume and their beauty. To become a queen is to become mortal.

Through the Looking-Glass continues the adventures of a character we know from an earlier book, enmeshing Alice in a process that transcends the more playful "nonsense" of *Alice in Wonderland* to the same degree that the story of Huckleberry Finn transcends the simple picaresque of *Tom Sawyer*. *The Snark* is much more intellectual and impersonal than either of the Alice books. Its dramatis personae consists of ten characters, all of whom are identified by titles or words that begin with the letter "b": Bellman, Boots, Bonnet Maker, Barrister, Broker, Billiard-mark-

er, Banker, Beaver, Baker, and Butcher. It is clear that
this swarm of "b's" represents "*being*," just as it is
clear from the subtitle—"An Agony in Eight Fits"—
that a death will occur. The object of the big-game
hunt, the Snark, lives on a remote island to which the
characters sail, again conjuring up associations with
the *Odyssey*, the mountain of Purgatory Ulysses
glimpses in the *Divine Comedy*, and all other islands
of romance or satire.

But Carroll deliberately reduces the sailing portion
of his text to a minimum, perhaps in order to diminish
his poem's overt dependence on its literary progenitor,
Apollonius of Rhodes's *Argonautica*. Seizing the Gold-
en Fleece, assembling a crew of heroes, charting a
course through the mythological geography of the Hel-
lenistic world: The mere depiction of these actions
makes Apollonius as much the hero of his poem as Jason himself. That is, every aspect of the *Argonautica* is
a literary challenge whose successful termination
makes the reader applaud the author. It is no wonder,
then, that Apollonius does not bother to develop his
characters in psychological terms and that Jason himself is a shadowy, low-relief figure.

This idea of competition between author and character as presences in the poem reappears in *The Snark*.
We know nothing, for instance, about the Bellman,
who is not a Jason figure but a Hermes leading souls to
the place where being is put to the test. About the
other important characters, the Butcher, the Beaver,
the Barrister, and the Baker, we know only how they
react to the hunt itself. The hunt, the gratuitous game
they play to increase their being, is dangerous and, like
Alice's participation in the chess game, tainted with
sensuality. Playing the chess-life game leads Alice into
sexuality, and the hunt stimulates passions: One of the
names for Dionysus is "Zagreus," "The Great Hunter," an epithet that underlines the connection between

hunting and incontinent, insatiable desire. The relationship between games, the hunt as blood sport, and the pursuit of objects of desire is the central issue of *The Snark*, although this issue undergoes several metamorphoses. That is, being versus nonbeing, loss of identity through passion, and loss of identity through the pursuit of fame—the writer's absorption by his own texts—are all metaphors for one another.

All of these versions of loss make *The Snark* a long meditation on the idea of subtraction. This mathematical drama derives from Humpty Dumpty's demand that Alice write down her assertion (originally his) that 365 minus 1 equals 364. When Alice hands him the problem, he turns it upside down, turning the subtraction into addition. Humpty Dumpty wants to avoid loss, even here where it is demonstrated that an individual has more un-birthdays than birthdays, at all costs. This arithmetic lesson is echoed in *The Snark* in Fit the Fifth: The Beaver's Lesson. In this chapter, the Butcher turns from violent dunce into sensitive wit and demonstrates to the pacific Beaver that 2 plus 1 equals 3. The Butcher's tautological demonstration reflects his relationship with the Beaver: From being two isolated individuals, antagonists in fact since the Butcher announces he "can only kill Beavers" (*Annotated Snark*, p.44), they become, like Lear's Owl and Pussycat, a loving, asexual couple.

The hunt ends happily for them, but only because they suppress passion, renounce violence, and live in a perpetual student-teacher relationship—with the Butcher as pedagogue. Their friendship is cemented when the Butcher identifies the Jubjub bird (also from "Jabberwocky"): "a desperate bird/Since it lives in perpetual passion" (*Annotated Snark*, p.72). By rejecting passion, symbolized by the Jubjub, the two become one: "In winter or summer, 'twas always the same—/ You could never meet either alone" (*Annotated Snark*, p.74). The opposite is true of the Banker, who also meets one of the animals from "Jabberwocky." His error is to yield to passion, which, as the narrator observes, makes him rush "madly ahead." He goes, literally, too far and is attacked by a Bandersnatch. The attack, again, is not fatal, but he loses his wits and his identity. He also loses the ability to communicate and ends up sitting in a chair chanting "words whose utter inanity proved his insanity/While he rattled a couple of bones" (*Annotated Snark*, p.84) He is reduced from one to zero.

The poem's only successful overreacher is never really present: the Snark itself. When the Bellman and the crew discuss the Snark, they define it as food. In fact, the Bellman tries to cheer up the crew after their arrival at the rather dismal island of the Snark with a list of the Snark's attributes:

> The first is the taste
> Which is meager and hollow, but crisp:
> Like a coat that is rather too tight in the waist,
> With a flavour of Will-o' the wisp.
>
> (*Annotated Snark*, p.51)

To this the Banker adds that in his dreams he serves Snark with greens (p.58). A Snark is a snack, a bite to eat, unless the Snark turns out to be a Boojum, in which case the diner becomes the dinner. As we live we consume, until our consumption consumes us: The more we add to ourselves the closer we come to nothingness. The wisdom we acquire after succumbing to temptation is costly indeed.

This combination of arithmetic (addition as subtraction) and eschatology appears in Carroll's preface to *The Snark*, where he ironically defends himself against the charge of having written nonsense: "I will not (as I might) point to the strong moral purpose of this poem itself, to the arithmetical principles so cautiously inculcated in it, or to its noble teachings in Natural History" (*Annotated Snark*, p.33). Caution is a very important aspect of the text: The Snark is always, as the Bellman and the narrator say, to be sought "with care," and the entire poem is in the mode of a cautionary tale. But it is the act of reading that must be exercised with the utmost caution because Carroll loads his allegory with so many possibilities that he renders interpretation itself a Snark hunt.

The "Barrister's Dream" (Fit the Sixth), a fantasy within a fantasy, is a parody of overinterpretation. The Barrister (not unnaturally) dreams of a courtroom in which the Snark defends a missing—actually dead—pig accused of deserting his sty. The Snark is a master of doubletalk:

> The fact of Desertion I will not dispute;
> But its guilt, as I trust, is removed
> (So far as relates to the cost of this suit)
> By the Alibi which has been proved.
>> *(Annotated Snark*, p.78)

Thus the pig is guilty and innocent at the same time. This trading in linguisitic surplus, where language adds to the facts, reappears a few stanzas later when the Snark agrees to summarize the case for the judge (who, oddly enough, had never done that before):

> So the Snark undertook it instead,
> And summed it so well that it came to far more
> Than the Witnesses ever had said!
>> *(Annotated Snark*, p. 78)

The presence of the Snark in the process makes the summation yield a total greater than the actual number of facts in the case. This rhetorical overload literally overflows when the Snark, acting as judge and jury, sentences his client the pig to be transported—exiled. The suddenly rigorous Snark is aghast to learn that "the pig had been dead for some years" (*Annotated Snark*, p.80). Thus, while the intervention of the Snark in the summation seems at first to produce a surplus—and does at the level of language—it actually produces a dearth: The wayward pig is condemned to involuntary removal from his sty, that is, to repeat against his will what he had done voluntarily. That banishment is, of course, nothing more than a metaphor for the death that has already taken place.

The only character who passes into nothingness in *The Snark* is the Baker, whose name (and profession) stand as a pun for "Maker," that is, for the poet or author. The other characters survive because they abandon the hunt, either because of madness (the Banker) or because of fraternal love and pursuit of scholarship (the Butcher and Beaver). The pursuit of immortality through works, the parody of the Renaissance writer's quest for immortality through writing, ends when the object of the hunt becomes the hunter. We may take the Baker as a figure for Lewis Carroll himself: The Banker forgets his name, and Dodgson so resented Lewis Carroll's fame that, at the end of his life, he returned all mail addressed to Lewis Carroll marked "Unknown."[10] The pursuit of immortality, of an undying name, ends in the creation of another name because the author's name comes to be something other than the name of the man. The mask replaces the author's mortal public face, but it is the mask that is real for others. If the fiction becomes more real than the man, the man runs the risk of becoming unreal, even to himself. This is exactly what happens: The disappearance of the Baker and the transformation of the Snark into the devouring Boojum are moments when the author confesses his loss of identity, the process whereby the manipulator of language is reabsorbed into the code he thought to dominate.

Lewis Carroll criticism constantly seeks to identify

Dodgson with his characters, especially Alice. The difference between that kind of identification of author and character and this identification of Carroll with the Baker is, simply, that the first wants to delve into the psychology of Charles Lutwidge Dodgson, to explain his celibacy, his love for little girls, and his eccentricities, while the second is merely interested in viewing *The Snark* as the swansong of Lewis Carroll, the author's lament about having played the literary game, having won, and having discovered that winning is losing, that Lewis Carroll became much more real than Charles Lutwidge Dodgson. The price of fame, like the wages of sin, is death: in this case, the fading of the heroic, conquistador author and the survival of the contemplative but less-gifted man.

The real protagonist of this *psychomachia* stands simultaneously inside and outside the creative process. It is as though Charles Lutwidge Dodgson were the mock-epic bard for Lewis Carroll, the Maker-Baker-Author. At the same time, Dodgson is Carroll's first reader and, by extension, all of Carroll's readers. The lessons learned through strife and temptation lead to wisdom, but the hero rarely benefits from his own experience. This is left to the reader, the ultimate survivor.

The Snark leaves the reader brooding over the disappearance of the Baker with a stanza that typifies the truncated, disjointed nature of mock-epic rather than the organic, cyclical epics Nohrnberg describes:

In the midst of the word he was trying to say,
In the midst of his laughter and glee,
He had softly and suddenly vanished away—
For the Snark *was* a Boojum, you see.

The poem mocks epic convention by ending *in medias res*, inverting the convention of the poet's invocation of the muse by addressing the reader, who must be understood as receiver of this eschatological action. The Baker dies with a word in his mouth, the word that identifies the object of his desire, now horribly transformed into his nemesis. The dark world closes in; there is no denouement, merely death and silence.

A more recent example of temptation epic leading to ultimate wisdom. of mock-epic used as displaced autobiography is Jorge Luis Borges's "Tlön, Uqbar, Orbis Tertius." Borges disguises his short story as a kind of personal statement: The narrator gives his version of a series of events. He even emends his account with a "Postscript of 1947" (totally false, the entire tale, including the postscript, was first published in 1940) in which he refers to his text as an "article."[11] This camouflaging technique is one of Borges's characteristic devices during the 1940s (the collections *Ficciones* and *El Aleph*), and would appear to be the ironic result of years of literary journalism.

In the late thirties, for example, Borges wrote a biweekly page entitled "Foreign Books and Authors" for *El Hogar* (Home), a Buenos Aires women's magazine. A peculiar feature of the page was the "synthetic biography" that accompanied translations or longer reviews of foreign books in which Borges would summarize as much information as he could discover about the life and works of a given author. This combination of book reviews and biography shapes Borges's aesthetics during the final years of the 1930s and all of the 40s: Already influenced by Marcel Schwob's *Imaginary Lives*, he could now turn to writing lives (building on what he had already done by rewriting the lives of real people in his 1935 book *A Universal History of Infamy*) of unknown or unreal people and reviews of imaginary books. The result in *Ficciones* (1944) and *El Aleph* (1949) would be stories such as "The Approach to Al-motasim," "Pierre Menard, Author of the *Quijote*,"

"Examination of the Works of Herbert Quain," and "Funes the Memorious." At the same time, he wrote stories of a thinly veiled autobiographical nature—"The South" is the most obvious example—and used himself as a character in other tales, such as "The Form of the Sword" and "The Other Death."

"Tlön, Uqbar, Orbis Tertius" occupies a place in Borges's oeuvre comparable to that of *The Snark* in Carroll's: Where Dodgson finds himself at odds with Lewis Carroll, Borges finds himself in discord with his own name. (This split between the man and the name is dramatized in the vignette "Borges and I" from *El Hacedor* [1960].) Where Dodgson has recourse to a second pseudonym or *persona* in order to represent his plight, Borges alludes to himself in his story by means of an absence: the total absence of his own name. It is as though he were putting into practice the riddle Stephen Albert proposes to Yu Tsun, the spy in "The Garden of Forking Paths," the riddle that is the clue to the central theme of Ts'ui Pen's labyrinthine novel:

[Stephen Albert] "In a riddle whose theme is chess, What is the only forbidden word?"
[Yu Tsum] "I reflected for a moment and answered: the word *chess*."
"Exactly," said Albert. "*The Garden of Forking Paths* is an enormous riddle or parable whose theme is time; that hidden cause prohibits any reference to the word. To omit one word *always*, to fall back on inept metaphors and obvious periphrases is perhaps the most emphatic way of pointing to that word."(*Ficciones*, p. 109)

"Tlön," then, is just this sort of allusion through exclusion: Borges uses the absence of his own name from the story to emphasize his presence within the story. All the while, the story deals with his ultimate disappearance.

The tale opens with a nocturnal *cena*, a dialogue

intended to recall the *Symposium* and the *Republic*, as well as a host of satiric literary dialogues, such as Oscar Wilde's *Decay of Lying*. Two literary men, the unnamed narrator and the novelist Adolfo Bioy Casares, discuss the possibility of writing "a first-person novel, whose narrator would omit or disfigure the facts and fall into diverse contradictions that would allow a few readers—very few readers—to intuit an atrocious or banal reality" (*Ficciones*, p.13). This literary conversation is cut short because its function, like that of the story's first word, "Debo" (I owe), a first-person verb, is to call attention to the idea of the first person as an unknown, possibly equivocating, entity. The narrator remarks on the menacing quality of mirrors, and his dining companion, Bioy Casares, responds with a quotation about mirrors that renders him the unwitting messenger of the creators of Tlön. Tlön is a mystery the narrator will attempt to resolve by embarking on an intellectual quest. Using Nohrnberg's diagram, we would locate the narrator of "Tlön" in the Quest Epic quadrant, out of which he moves into the Research Episode, to end in a dismal contemplation of final truths in the Wisdom Epic quadrant. The narrator passes on the burden of his knowledge to the reader, much in the way the narrator of *The Snark* mockingly addresses his reader in the last, death-fraught stanza of the poem.

The first person in "Tlön" also emphasizes the ironic relationship between the epic's third person and the first-person narrators of other narrative modes, particularly confessional and picaresque writing. The aristocratic aspect of epic, its professional singer dedicated to singing about heroes and heroic actions for an audience taught to identify itself with those figures and actions, would appeal to a Renaissance author, precisely because the concept of court poet justified the profession of poet. The epic poet is a character in his own poem (as he is in celebratory poems, such as odes and elegies) as the trope of invocation demonstrates: No one calls more attention to himself than a virtuoso performer asking for assistance.

The first-person narrator, despite the fact that he talks openly about himself, has humbler origins: Petronius's *Satyricon* parodies epic and romance conventions and seeks only to be comic. Saint Augustine humbles himself before God and allows the reader to witness the act. The *Confessions* is a serious parody of epic wherein the saint sings God's praises because God has made him immortal through grace, in contradistinction to the bard who sings the praises of the hero. *Lazarillo de Tormes* simultaneously satirizes the religious confession and the epic: Lazarillo must write his autobiography because a superior demands he does so and so that "such marvelous things, perhaps never before heard or seen, come to the attention of many, and are not buried in the grave of oblivion."[12] Lazarillo has a tale to tell, but he must be his own bard: His preface parodies Book 1 of the *Aeneid*, where Neptune saves Aeneas from drowning by calming the storm. Lazarillo states that he has had to make his own way, "rowing with force and guile" to a safe port. His life divides into two parts, a quest for identity (survival, a place in the world) and dissimulation (the discovery that the cost of securing an identity is self-respect). Lazarillo has a reason to write: To communicate his *desengaño*, yet another form of dark wisdom; not the enlightenment of the sinful man who discovers the folly of his ways, but the disillusion of the man who finds that the search for happiness has been a waste of time.

"Tlön" has *desengaño* of the kind Lazarillo experiences as well as irony at its core because it too is a futile quest in which the goals set at the beginning reappear at the end to mock the protagonist. "Tlön" differs from *The Snark* again, because it is a first-person narrative in that it is concerned more overtly with the psychological development of an individual and is, therefore, less abstractly allegorical. But "Tlön" too is a funerary monument of the spirit, an elegiac work, but of the most elliptical sort because the name of the person remembered is deliberately omitted. That the person commemorated and the narrator are one and the same person renders this literary act analogous to the unknown soldier's laying a wreath at his own tomb.

"Tlön" is difficult to read because of its camouflage, its disguises. It seems at first to be an anecdote ("How I discovered Uqbar"), as if someone asked the narrator to give an account of his experience in the way the narrator of "Funes the Memorious" is asked to contribute an essay to a volume on Funes or the way Lazarillo is asked (or compelled) to give an account of his life. As the story unfolds and the monstrous nature of what the narrator has discovered is revealed, it becomes less and less clear whether we can rely on the narrator—he may be mad. Naturally, the false postscript encourages the reader to think he too has lived through many of the experiences the narrator describes and that what he tells is not totally unfamiliar to us.

The narrator makes us privy to certain information related to the words in the title of his essay, information about how he came to know about them and how from words they became things. The first sentence of the story is charged with irony: "I owe the discovery of Uqbar to the conjunction of a mirror and an encyclopedia" (*Ficciones*, p.13). The first irony is the narrator's assumption that we know who he is, a mystery only circumstantially resolved. The second irony is that he assumes we know who or what Uqbar is; this is one of the "givens" of the entire narrative, that is, that we and the narrator share certain experiences.

The third irony involves the idea of discovery. The word carries with it the idea of a person who goes beyond established limits, a scientist, a Columbus, or, again, Dante's Ulysses. The enigma of discovery is the thing discovered: Is it something known or unknown? In scientific research, the discoverer embarks on a quest for something whose existence is supposed but unverified, an element or a cure. In literary discovery, the object of a quest may be the plant that confers immortality (as in the Gilgamesh epic), the Grail, or the Snark. The searcher may also seek wisdom or salvation, in which case the path to the goal serves as a learning or purifying process: The search either is the goal or is an important part of it. In Borges's story there is no physical quest, even though the narrator visits Uruguay: Knowledge comes unbidden to him. The "conjunction of a mirror and an encyclopedia" may seem fortuitous, but it is predestined. Like Oedipus, the narrator gathers information about a mystery, information actually about his own mysterious self.

The first sentence of the story juxtaposes four elements: the first person (again, only the verb is present; the pronoun is omitted), a mirror, an encyclopedia, and Uqbar. This one + three combination (the anonymous "I" and the three nouns) is in fact a chain of events in time: The mirror disturbs the narrator (mirrors have always disquieted Borges; he includes them in a list of "horrible imaginings" in a 1939 essay),[13] and this specular intromission causes Adolfo Bioy Casares (one of the many real people the story transforms into characters) to reinforce that loathing with a quotation. He lends the narrator's repugnance prestige by associating it with a statement by a heresiarch quoted in an encyclopedia article. The article deals with a place called Uqbar, but the heresiarch's declaration, that mirrors and copulation are abominable because they multiply the number of men, is actually taken from an earlier text by Borges himself.[14] The discovery is a recovery:

The past (the earlier book), rejected and put aside, returns to claim present reality. As in *The Snark*, what begins as a process of acquisition—the narrator's desire to find out just what the heresiarch, who is quoted from memory by Bioy Casares, "actually" said, to find out just where Uqbar is—ends as a process of reduction, of loss of being. The narrator's repressed past is a Boojum.

The narrator-protagonist of Borges's tale is a *pharmakos* who corresponds to the wisdom-seeking hero of epic. The game of conjunctions implies he is a randomly chosen victim, a sacrifice made to facilitate the entrance of Tlön into the real world. In fact he is not at all innocent, not at all the object of the wrath of the gods, not at all the sinful outsider who must be sacrificed in order for the community to survive. Like Oedipus, the narrator committed sins in the past: He created verbal systems, and now his monstrous machines, which he thought were locked away in "the tomb of oblivion," come back to haunt him and destroy his world.

The psychoanalytic possibilities of "Tlön" (like those of *The Snark*) are immense: The guilty narrator has repressed his past thoughts and writings—even the perverse false attribution of the quotation about mirrors and paternity to an imaginary heresiarch is an ironic repression as well as a clue to what the story is about—but these refuse to die. They come back disguised as the discourse of the "other,"as ideas confabulated by other thinkers, but they speak to and about the narrator. As Severo Sarduy says apropos of another self-reflecting text, "As in that other place without limits which is dreams, here everything says *I*."[15]

It is impossible not to identify the narrator of "Tlön" with Jorge Luis Borges. If we do, we may then apply this statement made by Borges in 1926 both seriously and literally:

This is my postulate: All literature is autobiographical in the last analysis. Anything can be
poetic provided it reveals to us a destiny, provided it
gives us a glimpse of one. In lyric poetry, this destiny
usually remains fixed, alert, but sketched in by sym-
bols that harmonize with its individuality and which
permit us to trace it back to its source....In novels the
same thing happens....It should be clear that I'm not
trying to deny the vitality of either drama or the
novel; what I'm asserting is our appetite for souls, for
destinies, for individualities, an appetite so knowl-
edgeable about what it seeks that if make-believe
lives don't satisfy it, it lovingly delves into the life of
the author. Macedonio Fernandez has stated all this
before.[16]

This manifesto-like "profession of literary faith" negates what Borges had postulated just one year earlier in
the essays of *Inquisiciones* (1925), where he denies the
existence of time, space, and the individual ego. Borges
is not only saying in 1926 that everything an author
writes reflects him in some way, but that the reason
why we read literature is to satisfy our hunger for souls
and destinies.

What the Borges of 1926 does not say is that each
book an author publishes constitutes a projected image
of himself, and that each successive book corrects or
negates the preceding image even as it projects a new
one. Thus each projection is accompanied by a repression, as the career of Borges himself illustrates: The
books he published during the twenties ceased to
please him by the forties, so he simply refused to re-
print them. The narrator of "Tlön" discovers that literature taken as autobiography or self-portrait is another
mirror, another horrible human invention, another reminder that identity is something we desire, repress,
and create. The identity we wish, subsequently, to de-

fine as alien, the self we reject, returns: Snarks always
turn into Boojums. The texts we produce to make our
name in the minds of others, for others to consume,
return to consume us.

The apocalyptic ending of the story is clearer if we
understand it as the logical result of the narrator's discovery that Tlön is his own past—his writings—which
has returned to deprive its creator of the chance to project more self-images. Nohrnberg's Quest Epic back-
fires on its protagonist, who finds himself, like the
Baker, the object of a hunt.

The "Postscript of 1947" transforms the quest into
the eschatological, contemplative wisdom epic because it contains the narrator's final perspective on
what has happened to him. It clarifies the first two
parts of the tale, the anecdotes about how the narrator
first makes contact, through Bioy Casares, with Uqbar,
and how the dead Herbert Asche is yet another link in
the sequence that allows the narrator to learn about
Tlön and its idealist reality. The postscript also describes the process by which human languages, history, and all the institutions that have been a part of
human society, generated, that is, as much by chance
as intention, are being replaced by those from Tlön,
which is a created world and therefore virtually devoid
of chance. Tlön is all intention.

The narrator, who had been present at most of the
interventions of the created world in human reality between 1935 and 1947, is alone in the postscript, a spectator instead of an actor. Here he speaks about the
future and the present—but not the past, the subject of
the first two parts of the tale, much as if he were the
soul of Anchises in Book 6 of the *Aeneid:*

Then English, French, and even mere Spanish will dis-
appear from the planet. The world will be Tlön. I
don't pay any attention and go on revising an inde-

cisive, quevedian translation (which I have no
intention of publishing) of Browne's *Urn Burial.*
(*Ficciones*, p. 37)

Faced with imminent disaster, a disaster he has in
some mysterious fashion brought into the world, the
narrator stands back and becomes a prophet. His own
being is shrinking and disappearing: Words, the articles
and encyclopedias written by the creators of Uqbar,
have displaced human life. The verbal systems the narrator once created to control reality have now become
reality.

The narrator is so close to death that he can work
only with dead versions of living languages, languages
that once were spoken and are now only antique publications. His exercise of translating one seventeenth-
century author into the idiom of another is comparable
to the carving of an ornate coffin which will be sealed
inside a pyramid. That is, the narrator disguises himself in the language of one dead author in order to
translate the words of another dead author, all in an
attempt to dissimulate the death that menaces him.

The theme of the text Borges chooses (he gives no
reason for translating Sir Thomas Browne, although he
had written on Browne as early as 1925 in *Inquisiciones* and had continually written on him throughout
the thirties) is immortality. This takes the form of perplexed meditation on some burial urns holding the
ashes of the dead but bearing no names, no personal
identification. Here we must see the narrator as Borges,
whose friends and ideas fill the story, at age forty deny-
ing his name to a text that will make him famous and
creating the idea of the anonymous text (Uqbar) composed by dozens of authors in order to destroy humanity. The passage quoted above is Borges's "last words,"
a farewell to philosophy and other forms of systematic

thought—which is mocked by Sir Thomas Browne's essay. Here is Browne, musing on the makers of those ancient urns:

Had they made as good provision for their names, as they have done for their relicks, they had not so grossly erred in the art of perpetuation. But to subsist in bones, and be but pyramidally extant, is a fallacy in duration.[17]

"Tlön" is Borges's urn: It contains his personality, especially the idealist philosopher Borges of 1925, and is made up of his ideas.

Like *The Snark*, "Tlön" is a theory of the writer's destiny: He sacrifices himself to explore the expressive possibilities of language. Thus the writer does not explore his own identity but instead gives his identity over to language, just as Charles Lutwidge Dodgson gave his identity over to creating Lewis Carroll. If the writer is successful, if his manipulations of language transform the way language is used—the most powerful effect a single user of the code can have on the code and on the others who use it—he will eventually fuse with the code. His style will become part of language. If an author, following the Renaissance *topos*, thinks he will achieve immortality through writing, he is creating a fiction that enables him to write. His name may survive, but no part of him will. His style over time will be reabsorbed by language and become public property. This idea finds expression in Borges's poignant vignette "Borges and I," from the suggestively titled collection *El Hacedor (The Maker)* (1960).

"Tlön" is a cautionary tale cut along Platonic or Nietzschean lines about the danger of fictions. There is great despair in it and great irony: The quest for immortality or wisdom consumes the protagonist's life. Again, like *The Snark*, "Tlön" is an agony. The greatest mockery for the living writer is the text he created in the past which he now repudiates, ignores, or seeks to rewrite. Like Frankenstein's nameless monster (who in the popular imagination has usurped his creator's name), it pursues the writer, mocking him. Unlike Proust, Borges here takes no joy in seeing this artifact pass before his eyes. The writer's exploration of language, his constant production of new texts, ends in repetition: Old texts return to haunt him, to remind him that they live on while he approaches his end.

The quest that leads to wisdom ends here in a demonic epiphany of futility: The verbal world created by the writer, loose in the real world, seduces readers into taking it for reality. The creator (Borges, in this case) recognizes the human frailty of his creation and writes a text about himself to illustrate it: the story of a man who stumbles onto a created world so attractive it convinces people to turn their backs on experienced reality in favor of verbal reality. Like the Baker, Borges (or his narrator, whoever he is) will "softly and suddenly vanish away," his pursuit of ideas, art, and a name swallowed by language. That the story is also a commentary on the world of 1940, a world at war because of ideology—words—is also true: The tragedy is not only personal but collective.

The mock epic, as exemplified by *The Snark* and "Tlön," deals with the horrors of human existence, especially the existence of the writer, in a seemingly humorous fashion. Lewis Carroll, incredibly, wrote his poem for children, and Borges's story was included in an anthology of fantastic literature, the kind usually labeled "escapist writing." Each brings its protagonist through a process that parodies the quest and which ends as a search for death. Wisdom is attained in the process, but at a cost that makes its acquisition of questionable value. These are, ultimately, epics of anguish, stories that touch the nerve of modern man's sense of what the meaning of life is. If all writing, as the Borges of 1926 suggests, is autobiographical, then all writing is a quest for identity that extinguishes its author. Language, the Boojum lurking at the end of all Snark hunts, devours its creator. He disappears, leaving behind nothing but words.

5

Epic Adumbrations: Carlyle, Hardy, da Cunha, and Vargas Llosa

In Book 6 of *The French Revolution* (1837), Thomas Carlyle defines his subject in satiric terms: "The 'destructive wrath' of Sansculottism: this is what we speak, having unhappily no voice for singing."[1] Carlyle's parody of the opening verses of the *Iliad* reflects the triumph of both the historian and the novelist over the epic poet in the nineteenth century. Carlyle mocks epic apparatus—the singing bard in this instance—in the same way Cervantes and later novelists mock the machinery of romance, whose idealized codes of behavior and stereotyped characters are at cross-purposes with the representation of reality.

There would seem to be no room for epic in an age avowedly intent on separating truth from myth, the age of Hegel, Darwin, and Marx. These men studied the past with an eye toward explaining both the present and the future; they were not intent on idealizing the past as, say, Virgil was, but on relating the past to the future. These nineteenth-century thinkers inverted Aristotle's notion about the superiority of poetic truth to historic truth—the general is always superior to the particular—because they and their century believed in a specific plot in history, one in which notions such as "progress" or "evolution" reinforced the belief that "civilization" was moving toward some utopian "higher state."

Carlyle, however, has another reason for alluding to epic in his history, one that mitigates the satire of the passage quoted above. In his final chapter, he notes:

Homer's Epos, it is remarked, is like a Bas-Relief: it does not conclude, but merely ceases. Such, indeed, is the Epos of Universal History itself. Directorates, Consulates, Emperorships, Restorations, Citizen-Kingships succeed this Business in due series, in due genesis on out of the other. (*French Revolution*, p. 725)

Carlyle espouses here a view of history quite unlike the progressive, evolutionary laws his age was promulgating. He finds, as had Machiavelli in his commentary on Livy, a swirling, cyclical pattern that moves from democracy to anarchy to authoritarian rule, a pattern devoid of evolution, with no ascent of a platonic stairway to wisdom. It holds no utopia of any kind.

As he chronicles these governmental successions, Carlyle is both passionate and objective: He may lament the rise and fall of governments, but in every instance he seeks to define a phase of history and to explain why it must give way to another as entropy robs it of vitality. The objectivity and drama of the Homeric narrator is clearly a role Carlyle envies and imitates even as he takes epic conventions to task. Carlyle admires Homer's ability to describe human conflict with passion but without sentimentality, Homer's ability to see that however grand in scale those actions are, they are nevertheless contained within the structure of fate.

When Richard Garnett assesses *The French Revolution* in his *Life of Thomas Carlyle* (1887), he speaks of it both as history and as epic:

There remains *The French Revolution*, a work which, if we regard it as a history, marks an epoch in historical composition from which literary annalists will date; which, as a poem, should not be less certain of immortality than its weaker, though strong, forerunner, Lucan's *Pharsalia*.[2]

Thus both Carlyle and his elegant biographer link *The French Revolution* with epic, but Garnett goes on to add another genre when he describes Carlyle's narrative technique:

Other historians gave the Revolution at secondhand, but he at firsthand. That peculiar feeling of reality, as if one's own blood bounded with the emotion of the event, which others have successfully called up in detached scenes, as Schiller in his description of the battle of Lutzen, Carlyle excited throughout a long history. The secret was his power of such thorough identification with the feelings of the actors in the occurrences that the reader felt a hearer, and the hearer felt a witness, and the witness seemed well-neigh an actor in the impassioned drama. (*Garnett*, pp.82-83)

Carlyle's text, then, combines history, epic, and drama:History because it is about events that actually happened, epic because, like the *Iliad*, it recounts the end of a dynasty in highly charged language, and drama because of Carlyle's use of dialogue and apostrophe together with his skill in recreating a scene from various points of view. At no time does either Carlyle or Garnett mention the word "novel," an absence as significant as the presence of the three genres they do mention.

Hayden White, in *Metahistory: The Historical Imagination in Nineteenth-Century Europe*, evaluates Carlyle's contribution to historiography in this way:

Carlyle, in short, possessed a critical principle, one that singled out the individual hero, the man who accomplishes something *against* history, as the proper object of a humanly responsible historiography. The "Chaos of Being," which Constant apprehended as a horrifying void and which Novalis viewed as an undifferentiated plenum of vital forces, was conceived by Carlyle to be the *situation* the heroic individual faces as a field to be dominated, if only temporarily and in the full knowledge of the ultimate victory this "Chaos" will enjoy over the man who seeks to dominate it. "History," in Carlyle's thought, was endowed with greater inherent meaning than it possessed in Constant's apprehension of it. And human life is endowed with greater value precisely to the degree to which the individual takes it upon himself to impose form upon this "Chaos," to give to history the mark of man's own aspiration to be something more than *mere* chaos.[3]

This struggle between the "Chaos of Being" (an expression Carlyle uses in his essay "On History") and the exceptional man or hero reflects the struggle between the historian and his subject. In a modality reminiscent of Ortega y Gasset's Existentialist summation of life as a struggle between man and his circumstances (in *Meditations on the Quijote*), the historian is also a species of hero: He salvages the biographies of great men from the chaos of history. Research then is a kind of mortal combat.

This is a strange idea in the context of nineteenth-century historical and novelistic narration where the narrator is usually a detached observer who either accumulates causes and effects or already has them in hand. Carlyle, unlike Balzac, is not a secretary to history: He is alternately its satiric bard and a sort of squire to those great men who seek to make history over in their own image. Among those great men Carlyle includes poets, as this statement from "The Hero as Poet" demonstrates:

August Wilhelm Schlegel has a remark on his
[Shakespeare's] Historical plays, *Henry Fifth* and the
others, which is worth remembering. He calls them a
kind of National Epic . . . There are really, if we look
to it, few as memorable Histories.[4]

For Carlyle, Shakespeare and Dante are heroes because
they are the voice of a national spirit: The hero-poet is
a secular prophet.

In Book 6 of *The French Revolution*, Carlyle describes the world as a scene of constant "revolution
and mutation" (p. 167) and concludes that the "French
Revolution means here the open violent Rebellion, and
Victory, of disimprisoned Anarchy against corrupt
worn-out Authority" (p.167). Where he differs from
Machiavelli is in his idea of the cycles of history: Instead of a simple return to authority from anarchy,
Carlyle sees in anarchy the seeds of a "new Order,"
that is, not merely a reconstituted form of the old order
but something different. Thus the circle turns into an
open spiral as history follows its course. These spatial
metaphors are significant because they signal Carlyle's
intentions with regard to his subject, as we see here in
his essay "On History":

For as all Action is, by its nature, to be figured as
extended in breadth, and in depth, as well as in
length; that is to say, is based on Passion and Mystery, if we investigate its origin; and spreads abroad on
all hands towards completion, so all narrative is, by
its nature, of only one dimension; only travels forward towards one, or towards successive points:
Narrative is *linear*, Action is *solid*.[5]

Carlyle's metaphor of history-writing resembles Saussure's notion of synchronic linguistics in that Carlyle
recognizes that linear history-writing, with its chains
of cause and effect falsifies and simplifies the historical

process. To understand a historical moment (or a linguistic moment in Saussure's sense), it is necessary to examine all the elements that constitute it. As Philip Rosenberg puts it, "In it [Carlyle's historical writing] linear narrative is replaced by the polycentric perspective of a sociological sense of history; throne-rooms and assembly halls as scenes of decision-making give place to the streets as a scene of action; and rational order is annihilated by the potency of the irrational."[6]

Carlyle's techniques produce a bizarre text: It is doubtless a history, but because it appropriates aspects of epic and drama, it extends beyond whatever the limits might be of history-writing. To read Carlyle we must judge him by the standards he sets for himself, this above and beyond his veracity, his reproduction of the "facts." This in itself is strange, because we usually judge historians by other means—by comparing their interpretation of events with that of others, or by how they have made use of information. It may be, and in reading Carlyle in the late twentieth century it certainly seems the case, that we ought to read *The French Revolution* according to other codes, more as a monument in the history of culture than as an explanation of the French Revolution. But if we do, we must decide by which code we are judging it. This would have to be some amalgam of epic and drama, fiction as opposed to "nonfiction."

Because of Carlyle's belief in historical necessity and his sense of the inevitability of entropy, we might consider locating him in the context of satire. Another reason would be his self-conscious attack on epic, which situates him, as it were, above his subject, in a vantage point that allows him to feel superior to what is below. This phenomenon often appears in "realistic" literary texts, *Madame Bovary*, for example. There, just when we suppose we are following characters who are "just like us," we find Flaubert satirizing them. His use of

Corneille's statue in the first chapter of Part 3, for instance, constitutes an allusion to tragedy in the grand style, not what we read in his history of a provincial lady infatuated after having read a few silly books.

There are many kinds of satire, but the type that concerns us here is related to tragedy—to wars, the collapse of dynasties, and the destruction of cities. In the third essay of the *Anatomy of Criticism*, "Archetypal Criticism: Theory of Myths," Northrop Frye discusses the relationship between irony and satire under the heading "The Mythos of Winter". For Frye, irony is an aspect of literary attempts "to give form to the shifting ambiguities and complexities of unidealized existence-" (*Anatomy*, p.223). The disparity between the real and the ideal, according to Frye, creates an "ironic myth" which is a "parody of romance: the application of romantic mythical forms to a more realistic content which fits them in unexpected ways" (*Anatomy*, p.223). We might recall that Frye links four abstract emplotments of human existence with the four seasons: comedy with spring, romance with summer, tragedy with autumn, and irony-satire with winter. The extremes tend to blend: Comedy touches and blends with both satire and romance, while romance joins with comedy and tragedy. Similarly, tragedy may tend toward romance and irony.

This final distinction is of great importance to this discussion of literary attitudes towards history. When tragedy falls under the influence of irony, it does so, Frye says, in two phases. First, as in much Shakespearean tragedy, the tragic situation is viewed from the perspective of experience (as opposed to romantic ideals), so that the tragic hero is a human being brought down by his own errors and is not a demigod destroyed by fate. A romance element is still present in this phase, but it disappears when tragedy falls under the sign of irony. Here, as in Carlyle's description of the process of French history quoted above, the author is primarily concerned with chronicling a natural process, the constant revolving of the wheel of fortune. Frye makes a comparison that comes directly to the point of this essay:

Like the corresponding phase of tragedy, it [fatalistic tragedy] is less moral and more generalized and metaphysical in its interest, less melioristic and more stoical and resigned. The treatment of Napoleon in *War and Peace* and in *The Dynasts* affords a good contrast between the fourth and fifth phases of irony. (*Anatomy*, p.237)

Where Tolstoy is concerned with locating the Napoleonic wars and Russian history in the realistic, essayistic (his text concludes with an essay on history) world of the novel, Hardy deals with the Napoleonic wars and English history from the point of view of destiny.

Frye's distinction between Hardy and Tolstoy reminds us that Carlyle's epic sense of history, as it appears in *The French Revolution*, shaped by the author's belief that entropy conditions all human institutions is radically different from other kinds of history writing, especially those that idealize either the past or the future at the expense of the present. The difference between Carlyle and Hardy is the difference between the satirist and the ironist. Both render their subject abstract, unlike the novelist Tolstoy, yet both do so in different ways. Here is Carlyle *in nuce*:

How such Ideals do realize themselves; and grow, wondrously, from amid the incongruous ever-fluctuating chaos of the Actual: this is what World-History, if it teach any thing, has to teach us. How they grew; and after long stormy growth, bloom out mature, supreme; then quickly (for the blossom is brief) fall into

decay; sorrowfully dwindle; and crumble down, or
rush down, noisily or noiselessly disappearing.
(*French Revolution*, p.10)

Even here, in sentences that promulgate a theory of entropy in human ideals, the satiric humorist ("noisily or
noiselessly") is present: This element marks the difference between Carlyle and Hardy.

If we think we know how to read Carlyle because his
book is entitled *The French Revolution: A History* and
subsequently discover that if we really do intend to
read it we must take other narrative forms into account (breaking down in the process the distinction between "fiction" and "nonfiction"), we have an even
harder time as readers with Hardy's *The Dynasts*
(1903-8). In his preface, Hardy constantly speaks of *The
Dynasts* as a "Spectacle" or as a "Drama," although he
had already been criticized for doing so, as he notes:

Readers will readily discern, too, that *The Dynasts* is
intended simply for mental performance, and not for
the stage. Some critics have averred that to declare a
drama [Hardy called it an "Epic-drama" in a note of
1909] as being not for the stage is to make an an-
nouncement whose subject and predicate cancel each
other. The question seems to be an unimportant matter of terminology....To say, then, in the present case,
that a writing in play-shape is not to be played, is
merely another way of stating that such writing has
been done in a form for which there chances to be no
brief definition save one already in use for works that
it superficially but not entirely resembles.[7]

Hardy's self-defense is another sad chapter in the im-
poverished history of literary genres, where genres are
either procrustean beds or meaningless abstractions.
Ideally, a generic designation is a summary of the hints
the critic has gleaned from the text itself on how it
wants to be read. The matter of definition is, of course,

crucial—unless we wish to reenact Humpty Dumpty's sermon on the meaning of words—but it is also important to remember that to call a text a novel or an epic-drama is to point out those traits we think dominant in it, even if the book shares traits with texts belonging to other genres.

Critics have long taken note of the epic qualities in Hardy's novels, the "abstract" qualities of a Tess or a Jude that R. J. White, for example, uses to link those characters to Milton, Shakespeare, or even Bunyan.[8] White falls back on the tradition that declares genius (Hardy in this case) free to make its own rules:

At the head of his last major work of fiction Hardy wrote the words, THE LETTER KILLETH. The phrase might fitly stand at the head of any essay on Hardy as a man of letters, for the utterance of all that lay behind his unique temperament was unlikely ever to find itself in any of the established forms of literature. In the end he was obscurely aware of this. What he sought to achieve in *The Dynasts* was a vast shadow-show of destiny, a complex of song and dance and mime which should project into the mind of the reader the realities which lie behind appearance. (White, p.18)

White's dependence on biography, history, and the vestiges of the Romantic tradition reflect a kind of literary criticism that has come under serious scrutiny in recent decades. Even supposing we had no serious argument with White's conclusions, we might wonder about his supposition that Hardy's genius not be expected to express itself in "the established forms of literature." White seems to be thinking of the novel as he says this, but there are literary forms—well-established ones—that resemble *The Dynasts* but that White does not discuss. Goethe's *Faust* is, after all, a drama, suitable only for "mental performance." There is as well the example of Seneca's tragedies, performed, to be sure, but also of an abstract, idealized nature. Goethe and Seneca remind us of yet another theatrical tradition, one that oscillates between stage performance and mental recitation: Spanish baroque drama, especially that of Calderón, which Romantic literary critics, the Schlegel brothers in particular, rediscovered and proffered as models.

Northrop Frye has also used Calderón, his *autos sacramentales* especially, to define a genre he calls the "myth-play" (*Anatomy*, p.282), a drama that "emphasizes dramatically the symbol of spiritual and corporeal communion. The scriptural plays themselves were associated with the festival of Corpus Christi, and Calderón's religious plays are explicitly *autos sacramentales* or Eucharist plays" (*Anatomy*, p.282). Frye carefully points out that the myths these dramas deal with are already well known to the audience, and that at one level, therefore, they may be thought of as popular literature, even though they are quite esoteric. In any case, they are a theater of spectacle, neither tragic nor comic but ritualistic. Frye links Elizabethan masque with the myth-play, where the central myth is national identity, usually represented by the monarch. In this sense, Shakespeare's history plays are individual scenes in a huge masque that culminates in *Henry VIII* with the birth of Elizabeth l.

If that masque cycle ends on a comic note, there is another, ironic side to the tradition. As Frye says, "As we move further away from comedy, the conflict [between virtue and vice, good and evil] becomes increasingly serious, and the antimasque figures less ridiculous and more sinister. . . . This is the stage represented by *Comus*, which is very close to the open conflict of good and evil in the morality play. With the morality play we pass into another area of masque which we shall here call the archetypal masque" (*Anatomy*, p.290). This is the context in which we should locate *The Dynasts*, the archetypal masque in which Hardy rehearses the collapse of European culture because of its bizarre yoking of ideals and ambitions. Where Carlyle can smile in his review of the past, Hardy, writing at the end of the long international peace that ran, with slight interruptions, from 1814 to 1914, uses history as a prophetic book: He is composing an apocalypse.

History in *The Dynasts* is a process out of control. Where Carlyle detects the ebb and flow of power, the presence or absence of heroes, the life and death of ideals, Hardy finds only chaos. We see this in his use of otherworldly or superhuman agencies to comment on the action at hand, the Napoleonic campaigns. Hardy does not explain in his preface why he feels he has to include these presences, but it is clear he has epic machinery in mind—even though he realizes that machinery is outmoded. In this passage he comments ironically about his superhuman forces and those in epic:

The wide prevalence of the Monistic theory of the Universe forbade, in this twentieth century, the importation of Divine personages from any antique Mythology as ready-made sources or channels of Causation, even in verse, and excluded the celestial machinery of, say *Paradise Lost*, as peremptorily as that of the *Illiad* or the *Eddas*. And the abandonment of the masculine pronoun in allusions to the First or Fundamental Energy seemed a necessary and logical consequence of the long abandonment by thinkers of the anthropomorphic conception of the same. (*Dynasts*, pp. xxiv-xxv)

He is as unable to invoke the muses and Apollo as he is to call on the Judeo-Christian God. In place of gods, God, or even destiny, Hardy's spirits converse about the workings of the Immanent Will, a vision of the spinning out of cosmic energy curiously analogous to art for art's sake or to the idea of the nonrepresenta-tional in the plastic arts. Here the Spirit of the Years describes how the Immanent Will functions:

> It works unconsciously, as heretofore, Eternal
>   artistries in Circumstance,
> Whose patterns, wrought by rapt aesthetic rote,
> Seem in themselves its single listless aim,
> And not their consequence.
>
> (*Dynasts*, p.1)

The absence of a *telos* permits the free play of indi-vidual wills in a struggle of all against all that bears some resemblance to Schopenhauer's concept of will in nature, a blind force that works without any end or purpose.

Hardy anticipated such associations and ends *The Dynasts* on a note of hope. The "Semichorus I of the Pities" asks a question that repeats the question the "Shade of the Earth" asks at the beginning of the work: Both inquire into the workings of the Immanent Will. The end of the epic-drama suggests that the Will shall some day cease to be unconscious of its actions, that "Consciousness the Will informing, till It fashion all things fair!" (*The Dynasts*, p.525). This sounds like bad faith on Hardy's part, as if he imagines his readers un-able to tolerate the thought of an irrational force mov-ing the universe along through time, but it appears he did entertain the idea that the Will might become self-aware. He says so in a letter to Mr. Edward Wright con-cerning the philosophy of *The Dynasts*. The letter ap-pears in Florence Emily Hardy's *The Life of Thomas Hardy*, written in the main by Hardy himself:

In a dramatic epic—which I may perhaps assume *The Dynasts* to be—some philosophy of life was neces-sary, and I went on using that which I had denoted in my previous volumes of verse (and to some extent prose) as being a generalized form of what the thinking world had gradually come to adopt, myself included. That the Unconscious Will of the Universe is growing aware of Itself I believe I may claim as my own idea solely—at which I arrived by reflecting that what has already taken place in a fraction of the whole (i.e. so much of the world as has become conscious) is likely to take place in the mass; and there being no Will outside the mass—that is, the Universe—the whole Will becomes conscious thereby: and ultimately, it is to be hoped, sympathetic.[9]

The parenthetical "it is to be hoped" obliges the reader to speculate about Hardy's sincerity. Walter Wright[10] and others have pointed out that Hardy, for all his pessimism, loved life, that his worldview, though including some elements similar to the ideas of Schopenhauer, is not really nihilistic.

Hardy criticism too often confuses the philosophy of the man with the philosophy of the text. That is, *The Dynasts* is a strife-epic about the fall of a particular hero—Napoleon. It is also apocalyptic because, while it deals with the period of the Napoleonic wars, it is also darkly concerned with the present and with wars to come. In this sense it is a precursor of Virginia Woolf's last book *Between the Acts* (1941), a satiric novel that contains a pageant made up of scenes from British history up to the present, the early phase of World War II. The question Woolf raises is whether there will be a future English history; the question raised in *The Dynasts* is, Why should England have a future?

This is the burden of the epic writer, the problem that writer confronts in the nineteenth and twentieth centuries and answers in several ways. The writers under consideration here, Carlyle, Hardy, Euclides da Cunha, and Mario Vargas Llosa, have great difficulty finding ultimate justifications. Their texts therefore are tinged either with satire (Carlyle) or tragic irony

(Hardy). Their secret justification is the post-Romantic interpretation of the *topos* of immortality through writing: As artists they are mysteriously conscious of the meaning of history and must commit that knowledge to writing, the writing of allegorical fictions and not the direct writing of history. This explains why the figure of the artist looms large in all these texts, until, in Vargas Llosa, he becomes the central character.

The parallels between the historical essays of Carlyle and Euclides da Cunha and the fictions of Hardy and Mario Vargas Llosa are striking. In the case of Carlyle and Euclides, the reader is immediately struck by their shared tendency toward drama, their desire to transcend the printed word and make prose into theater. This theatricality is not at all like Hardy's drama, which in fact renders the action of *The Dynasts* static. Hardy's concept of theater is really operatic and informs the reader that he should take the text as symbolic action. This technique is echoed at the level of theme in Vargas Llosa, whose recreation of the Canudos campaign in late nineteenth-century Brazil reads like an account of a war in another world. Hardy and Vargas Llosa make the very real history they describe totally abstract.

And despite Carlyle's fascination with "great men" in history, *The French Revolution* is redolent of nihilism. That is, each phase of history seems to Carlyle to embody a particular will: Each has its moment of strength and then it decays. Ascribing permanence to any single moment or energy would be futile since all are mortal. That Carlyle would be fascinated by the individual who embodies the spirit of an age is not outrageous: Nor is it a scanting of the importance of the masses or groups whose interests the leader's will personifies. Carlyle was heir to the Romantic tradition and shares many of the ideas of his contemporaries.

This same notion—the individual's conformity with

his age—applies as well to Euclides da Cunha, a product of the positivism that shapes the intellectual life of nineteenth-century Latin America. Positivism sanctions the regime of Porfirio Diaz (1830-1915) in Mexico and enables the Argentine politician and man of letters Domingo Faustino Sarmiento (1811-88) to write his devastating interpretations of miscegenation in the Argentine Republic. It is in fact Sarmiento's 1845 masterpiece *Civilization and Barbarism; Life of don Facundo Quiroga* that provides Euclides with the format for *Os Sertões (Rebellion in the Backlands)* (1902). Sarmiento's text combines ethnography (the racial mixture that produces the Argentine gaucho) with biography (Facundo, the prototypical gaucho) and environmental psychology (the effect of geography and climate on the inhabitants of a particular place).

Where they differ is in Sarmiento's use of positivist thinking as ideological underpinning for his politics and in his concern with an individual, Facundo Quiroga. Euclides is concerned with an event, the destruction of a backwoods community, and how that event relates to the ethnic composition of the inhabitants of that community. Euclides and Sarmiento inevitably repeat each other: Both are determinists as far as race and environmental influence are concerned; and both are pessimists as far as the future intellectual and social development of mixed-blood societies is concerned. Both Sarmiento and Euclides are racists, by late twentieth-century standards. They believe in the superiority of the "white" race and in the inevitable triumph of that race. At the same time, both admire the mestizo people who are the antagonists in the struggle they depict.

This loathing mixed with admiration provides the tension that runs through both Sarmiento and Euclides, a tendency that renders their writing ambiguous. It is this ambiguity that saves their two books from having merely circumstantial or historical value. Like Carlyle, Sarmiento and Euclides must be read not only as historians but as novelists. That is, the personality of the historian emerges as such an important aspect of the history he writes that we move from history into a allegorical self-portraiture—the confessional novel. This theme dominates Mario Vargas Llosa's reconstruction of *Rebellion in the Backlands* and is consistent with Romantic and post-Romantic ideas on the importance of the author as a personality independent of his writing. It is, of course, a notion that appears in the Renaissance as well, especially in epic writers. The conclusion of *Orlando Furioso* contains Ariosto's self-portrait, the exhausted artist who is barely able to keep all the threads of his story under control.

The image of the writer under pressure certainly applies to Euclides da Cunha. In fact, *Rebellion in the Backlands* constitutes a self-defeating quest for ultimate sources, as Euclides presents his subject from every conceivable perspective—geology, geography, race, religion, and politics. He could easily have adopted Carlyle's attitude and written a satiric account of the Canudos uprising, which was after all the revolt of an army of rustic illiterates following a messianic lunatic into the millennium. Carlyle's idea of the growth, flourishing, and decay of ideals is represented in parodic form in the Canudos campaign. Euclides is aware of this potential for the grotesque and does not avoid it. But he uses it only in such a way that the grotesque becomes either the pathetic or the heroic. Thus his description of the typical *jaguŋo* (backwoodsman) is misleading:

He does not have the flawless features, the graceful bearing, the correct build of the athlete. He is ugly, awkward, stooped. Hercules-Quasimodo reflects in his bearing the typical unprepossessing attributes of the weak. His unsteady, slightly swaying, sinuous gait conveys the impression of loose-jointednesss. . . . On foot, when not walking, he is invariably to be found leaning against the first doorpost or wall that he encounters.[11]

The reader is led to expect very little from such an individual, and yet, a paragraph later, Euclides describes him galvanized into action:

Through an instantaneous discharge of nervous energy, he at once corrects all the faults that come from the habitual relaxation of his organs; and the awkward rustic unexpectedly assumes the dominating aspect of a powerful, copper-hued Titan, an amazingly different being, capable of extraordinary feats of strength and agility. (*Rebellion*, p.90)

This self-contradictory style characterizes the entire book: the racial mixture that produces the *jaguᶇo* is a blend of "inferior" peoples; but those inferior peoples withstand an army and die faithful to their cause in a way that would honor the most "superior" human types. Social Darwinism becomes its own parody in Euclides' writing: Afraid that the inferior peoples will beat them, the superior peoples must become more brutal than their adversaries. Civilization must become barbarism in order to demonstrate its superiority. This perpetual contradiction renders *Rebellion in the Backlands* a most difficult text to define in ideological terms, despite the author's professed espousal of the values of "civilization."

Carlyle's paradoxical blend of satire and epic enables us to understand Euclides' enterprise. In his essay on the Paraguayan dictator Dr. Francia, Carlyle mockingly returns to his theme of heroism and authorship:

The confused South American revolution, and the set of revolutions, like the South American continent itself, is doubtless a great confused phenomenon;

worthy of better knowledge than men yet have of it. Several books, of which we here name a few known to us, have been written on the subject; but bad books mostly, and productive of almost no effect. The heroes of South America have not yet succeeded in picturing any image of themselves, much less any true image of themselves, in the Cis-Atlantic mind or memory.[12]

Were we to imagine that Euclides da Cunha and Mario Vargas Llosa were aware of Carlyle's statement, we might conclude that their books were attempts to fill the void he describes. Carlyle tries to vindicate Dr. Francia in his essay by pointing out that while from a constitutionalist's point of view his concept of government was an aberration, his dictatorship preserved order in Paraguay and saved the nation from chaos.

Carlyle paradoxically finds a hero—his essay could be a species of essayistic elegy for a fallen hero, the recently deceased Dr. Francia—where others see only a villain. The implication for Euclides and Vargas Llosa is clear: Do not seek your hero among the heroes offered by historians. Look instead for a heroic action, then seek the origins of that action among those who participated in it. This is what Euclides and Vargas Llosa do: They sidestep the Bolívars and San Martíns in order to find heroism in one of the most shameful wars of any time, the war of extermination waged by the Brazilian Republic between 1896 and 1897 against the community of Canudos and its messianic leader, Antonio Vicente Mendes Maciel, Antonio Conselheiro (Antonio the Counselor).

Neither author tries to make Antonio Conselheiro into the hero of a religious epic: He is no Godfrey of Bouillon; neither of our authors is a Tasso; and Canudos was only a Jerusalem for those who died protecting it. Nor were the ideas those benighted people espoused worthy of consecration by an epic author: No author can derive much grandeur from the belief that the Republic was Antichrist, that civil marriage was a sin, or that King Sebastian of Portugal would rise from the sea with his knights to liberate Brazil from the devil (the Republic).

Euclides writes knowing there is no single hero, no dominant idea that could make the defenders of Canudos into something greater than they were. Moreover, he fully believed those people were doomed by their very nature, by being a mixture of inferior races. And yet he finds in their defense of their Jerusalem a glory that turns folly into heroism, that transforms madness and fanaticism into a crusade. He finds, in the geography, geology, and ethnography of the Brazilian Northeast the same lesson repeated endlessly:

The martyrdom of man is here reflective of a greater torture, more widespread, one embracing the general economy of Life. It arises from the age-old martyrdom of Earth. (*Rebellion*, p. 48)

This is a desperate form of Darwinism mixed with a heavy dose of Hobbes, a vision of a world in which struggle is universal, where the battle of all against all extends to the sun itself. This definition of the universe as a vast machine for causing pain marks the difference between Euclides and Sarmiento. Sarmiento admires the gauchos, yet he demands their extermination. That extermination would be an act of will, a purification, not the result of a preordained process. Euclides sees natural and human history as a predetermined flow, as in this passage, in which he declares what the future of all mixed-blood peoples, especially those of the Brazilian Northeast, will be:

The first effects of various ethnic crossings are, it may be, initially adapted to the formation of a great race; there is lacking, however, a state of rest and equilibrium, which the acquired velocity of the march of the peoples in this century no longer permits. Backward races today, tomorrow these types will be wholly extinguished. Civilization is destined to continue its advance in the backlands, impelled by that implacable "motive force of history" which Gumplowicz, better than Hobbes, with a stroke of genius, descried in the inevitable crushing of weak races by the strong. (*Rebellion*, p.xxix)

The Canudos campaign for Euclides was a "crime and as such to be denounced" (*Rebellion*, p.xxx)—despite his statement on strong and weak races—because he saw Brazilians destroying in a political frenzy what he called "the very core of our nationality, the bedrock of our race" (*Rebellion*, p.464). Canudos could only be a grotesque clash of beliefs: martyrdom (Antonio Conselheiro and his disciples dying for their faith), sacrifice (the Republican fanatics sacrificing the religious zealots at the Republican altar), and suicide (the nation killing itself). Canudos for Euclides was Troy and he was its Homer.

Unlike the other authors considered here, Euclides da Cunha was a witness (or partial witness; he saw only the last few months of the campaign) of the actions he describes. This difference makes him more like Bernal Díaz del Castillo, a foot soldier who published his own version of Cortés's conquest of Mexico. or like one of our modern war correspondents. This idea of the writer-witness impressed Mario Vargas Llosa[13] because the central character of his novel strongly resembles Euclides: he is a myopic, asthmatic journalist who accompanies the ill-starred Moreira Cesar expedition to Canudos at the end of February, 1897. Vargas Llosa alters the facts of Euclides's life by having his protagonist pass through the battle lines in order to spend the last four months of the war—from June until the beginning of October, 1897—in Canudos. Vargas Llosa also adds the ironic touch of having his unnamed journalist break his glasses so that during his stay in Canudos he is virtually blind, a fitting rite of passage for the man who swears (*War*, p.341) he will write about the Canudos affair, tell the truth about what happened, and, more important, make sure the war is not lost in oblivion.

Vargas Llosa subverts the authority of his author-in-the-text by presenting the entire action much in the style Carlyle uses to describe the nature of historical events: "Narrative is *linear*, Action is *solid*" (see above, p.153). He does this by disrupting chronological sequence, having characters discuss events which for them have already taken place but which are in the future for the reader; in short, he transforms his narrative into a simultaneous totality instead of a linear series. This is not the "spatialization of narrative" Joseph Frank describes in his celebrated essay,[14] but an attempt to take the in-medias-res convention of epic to its baroque limits. No character. no witness can ever completely fathom the meaning of the events taking place around him, while at the same time no future historian can know what those events meant for those who experienced them. Vargas Llosa deliberately mixes events in order to transcend the linearity of narrative, to make the reader a witness to the degree an author's imagination and prose can make this possible. He attempts through temporal confusion what Carlyle tried to accomplish through theater.

Despite his tacit confession that the historical event is unknowable as a "thing in itself," Vargas Llosa establishes a hierarchy of verbal artists in *The War of the End of the World*, perhaps in order to restore to artists the prestige they once had as epic bards. The journalist, the Euclides da Cunha figure, is ugly, awkward, and, like Carlyle in *The French Revolution*, has "no voice for singing." But it is he who will be reborn after his rite of passage in Canudos as the epic-historian who will be at the apex of Vargas Llosa's hierarchy.

Below him is the deformed León de Natuba, Antonio Conselheiro's chronicler or evangelist who writes down, in order, as he says himself to "eternalize" them (p.456), every word the Prophet speaks. On a lower level is a circus dwarf, also deformed, also monstrous, who keeps the journalist alive in Canudos by reciting fragments of epics and romances (tales of the Knights of the Round Table, the Twelve Peers of France, and other heroic stories) that are part of the oral tradition of the backlands (see esp. pp.338 and 350). Thus the written epic and the epic-historian depend on an oral tradition (derived from a decayed, forgotten written tradition) and on a tradition that indiscriminately combines hagiography, saints' lives, the lives of heroes, and the conservation of the words of a leader-saint by a disciple.

But the redaction of heroic deeds is only one aspect of the activity that goes into the formation of the epic-historian's identity. For all these writers, from Carlyle onward, their enterprise is in itself a struggle: The act of composition is a battle, and victory is completing the text. It is as if there were a parallel epic for writers; that is, if we take what Euclides says seriously and accept that the Canudos campaign is a strife epic, we see that included in that epic is a quest-epic whose protagonist is the writer. Thus, the war between the disciples of Antonio Conselheiro and the Republic ends in the destruction of a city, while the artist's search takes him first to research and then to the wisdom that allows him to contemplate that action as a totality. His grasp of the action in its entirety allows him to present it in a coherent, aesthetically satisfying text. Mario Vargas Llosa is aware of this pattern and pushes his journalist through all its stages: First he is the cynical, parasitic journalist; then he is the blind spectator-sufferer who participates in the stench and terror of war; finally he is an enlightened survivor gathering information to prepare himself to write.

Mario Vargas Llosa is not the only person to have written about the Canudos war with the writer's epic struggle in mind. In 1920, the Scot Robert Bontine Cunninghame Graham published *A Brazilian Mystic, Being the Life and Miracles of Antonio Conselheiro*,[15] a book he cribbed from Euclides da Cunha's *Rebellion in the Backlands*. In his preface, Cunninghame Graham claims that it was Teddy Roosevelt who suggested he write about the backwoodsmen of Brazil, but it is clear that as soon as he had read Euclides he was drawn irresistibly to the Canudos affair. He may have seen the parallels between the life of the *jagunços* and the harsh, violent life of the ancient highlanders as well as the similarity between the religious fervor of Antonio Conselheiro's disciples and the unswerving faith of Cameronians. Sir Walter Scott (of *Waverly, Old Mortality*, and *Rob Roy*) also influences Cunninghame Graham's understanding of Canudos, but what is truly striking about *A Brazilian Mystic* is the author's sense of mission in writing it:

This kind of book is bound to find its way, and shortly, to an old bookstall, there to be sold with other bargains for a penny. . .for it treats of unfamiliar people and of a life unknown and unsuspected by the general. It is no matter, for he who writes a book writes for his own peculiar pleasure, and if he does not, he had better far abstain from writing. . . .If it is fated that my account of the Jagunço mystic should lie rotting in the rain upon a stall, so be it. . . .Shrivel or rot, it is all one to me. Just as the struggle is the thing worth struggling for and the result is a secondary affair, so is the writing of a book what matters to the writer of it, for he has had his fight. (*Brazilian Mystic*, pp.xi-xii)

This is a melodramatic statement, but it echoes the central theme of this chapter: Writing about war is itself a war. Mario Vargas Llosa took note of Cunninghame Graham's brilliant pastiche of Euclides da Cunha and paid him a special homage. We read in *A Brazilian Mystic*: "The Emperor's writ had as little force in the Sertão as had the King's beyond the pass of Aberfoyle in the days of Rob Roy" (p.48). In *The War of the End of the World*, Galileo Gall, a Scottish anarchist-phrenologist trying desperately to reach Canudos, thinks: "The Republic has as little force in Bahía as had the King of England beyond the Pass of Aberfoyle in the days of Rob Roy McGregor" (*War*, p.74). This is no coincidence; it is one epic-historic writer's homage to another.

Writers are also readers, and it is the act of reading that creates the meaning of the text, the precursors of the texts we read, and the tradition itself. The meaning of *The War of the End of the World* is not merely to be found in Cunninghame Graham or Euclides da Cunha. Its meaning involves Sarmiento, Hardy, and Carlyle, to say nothing of Mario Vargas Llosa himself, spectator of a century of almost continuous warfare, both civil and international. He found a struggle, a "Great Historical Calamity, or Clash of Peoples," as Hardy puts it in *The Dynasts*, in Euclides da Cunha. It was a war that decided nothing, that changed history not a bit: In short, it was a war whose only justification could be the books that have been written about it, books that stand as monuments to heroism and madness, books that chronicle the violent and glorious in mankind.

Conclusion

Apologies to the reader are by now surely superfluous. This is an eccentric book about eccentric authors and texts, but the only way to effect a comparative study of Latin American and Anglo-American authors is to link the out-of-the-ordinary authors from the center of the Western tradition with those whose geographic and linguistic origins condemn them to being outsiders.

Certainly a list of authors that contains Joseph Conrad (the chameleon author from a land as peripheral as any Latin American republic who yet manages to interpolate himself into the metropolitan tradition), Lewis Carroll, and William Godwin cannot be considered one that pays homage to the "Great Tradition." Even Auden in this book becomes strange: an English author who writes about a civil war in Spain in a way that leaves both his meaning and his intentions ambiguous. Carlyle is an eccentric no matter what his subject is, and Hardy's *Dynasts* must be one of the oddest books ever produced by a major author.

But this is what makes comparative literary study interesting: The strangeness of Latin American literature shows us just how many bizarre authors and texts we have in our own literary tradition. This, of course, is an extrapolation of Borges's idea that each writer—through his readers—creates his own precursors. The eccentricity of both the Latin Americans and their counterparts in the English-speaking world does not diminish because we find eccentricity at home: It makes us realize that the house of literature contains many mansions, that the wealth of the Western tradition, including Latin America, is vast and growing. I have tried in these essays to identify some of the subterranean currents running throughout our common culture.

Certain themes recur in this book: the notion that Latin American literature holds up a parodic mirror to the West, that autobiography is a factor in books we would hardly think autobiographical, and that writers of narrative are profoundly concerned with history both as story and as truth. History looms large in most of the books I have chosen for study: from Auden and Neruda meditating on the future of the Spanish Republic to Mario Vargas Llosa musing over a futile war that took place in a no-man's-land at the end of the last century. These books give the lie to critics who attack modern Latin American writers for not dealing with reality. All of them are concerned with human life— even Borges's inexhaustible tale "Tlön, Uqbar, Orbis Tertius"—but they refuse to resolve life's problems by falling back on ideology or blind faith. If these writers share any feature it is the belief that literature ought to raise more questions than it resolves. Writers are entitled to express their moral concerns in their writing, and critics ought to point out those concerns.

These essays are experiments in comparative reading, nothing more. They seek to point out the vitality of a tradition that seems to many to be falling into entropy.

Notes

Introduction

1. René Wellek and Austin Warren, *Theory of Literature*, third edition (New York: Harcourt, Brace and World, 1962), p.49.

2. Geoffrey H. Hartman, "Towards Literary History," *Beyond Formalism: Literary Essays 1958-1970* (New Haven: Yale University Press, 1971), pp. 356-57.

3. Harold Bloom, *The Anxiety of Influence: A Theory of Poetry* (New York: Oxford University Press, 1973).

4. Claudio Guillén, "Genre and Countergenre," *Literature as System: Essays Toward the Theory of Literary History* (Princeton: Princeton University Press, 1971, pp.135-38.

5. Northrop Frye, *Anatomy of Criticism: Four Essays* (Princeton: Princeton University Press, 1957). See especially "Rhetorical Criticism: Theory of Genres," pp. 243-337.

6. Mikhail Bakhtin, *Problems of Dostoevsky's Poetics*, ed. and trans. Caryl Emerson, intro. Wayne C. Booth, Theory and History of Literature, vol. 8 (Minneapolis: University of Minnesota Press, 1984). See especially "Characteristics of Genre and Plot Composition in Dostoevsky's Works," pp. 106ff. Of interest in this context is Clive Thomson's essay "Bakhtin's "Theory" of Genre," *Studies in 20th Century Literature* 9, no. 1, Special Issue on Mikhail Bakhtin, ed. Clive Thomson (Fall 1984): 29-40.

7. Ernst Robert Curtius, "Spain's Cultural Belatedness," *European Literature and the Latin Middle Ages*, trans. W. Trask (New York: Harper and Row, 1963), pp. 541-43.

8. Walter Benjamin, *Reflections: Essays, Aphorisms, Autobiographical Writings*, ed. and intro. Peter Demetz, trans. Edmund Jephcott (New York: Harcourt Brace Jovanovich, 1979), pp. 146-62.

9. See Emir Rodriguez Monegal's *El Boom de la novela latinoamericana* (Caracas: Editorial Tiempo Nuevo, 1972) and "The Boom: a Retrospective" (interview with Rodríguez Monegal), *Review 33* (September-December, 1984):30-36.

10. Hernán Vidal, *Literatura hispanoamericana e ideología liberal: surgimiento y crisis (una problemática sobre la dependencia en torno a la narrativa del Boom)* (Spanish American Literature and Liberal Ideology: Triumph and Crisis [Problematics of Dependence with Regard to the Narrative of the Boom]) (Buenos Aires: Ediciones Hispamérica, 1976):

otro arquetipo más concreto y humano del escritor: la de aquel que no se concibe como ser descuartizado entre cuerpo y espíritu, sino la del escritor que los une en la praxis revolucionaria y se piensa a sí mismo como un trabajador más de la cultura. Mientras tanto la narrativa del *boom* se ha transformado en el espectáculo conmovedor de escritores—y críticos—que buscan abandonar su piel liberal pequeño buerguesa, aspiran a dejar de ser lo que son, mientras otros ya han agotado sus fuerzas en esta lucha y se unen paulatinamente a la reacción. (p.112)

11. John Gledson. *The Deceptive Realism of Machado de Assis: A Dissenting Interpretation of 'Dom Casmurro,'* Liverpool Monographs in Hispanic Studies 3 (Liverpool: Francis Cairns, 1984).

12. Carlos Fuentes, Interview: "The Art of Fiction, LXVIII," *The Paris Review* 82 (Winter 1981): 151.

13. Wolfgang Iser, *The Act of Reading: A Theory of Aesthetic Response* (Baltimore: The Johns Hopkins University Press, 1978).

14. Hans Robert Jauss, "Literary History as a Challenge to Literary Theory," *New Literary History* 2 (Autumn 1970): 7-37. And: *Aesthetic Experience and Literary Hermeneutics*, trans. Michael Shaw, intro. Wlad Godzich, Theory and Histo-

ry of Literature, vol. 3 (Minneapolis: University of Minnesota Press, 1982).

15. E. D. Hirsch, *Validity in Interpretation* (New Haven: Yale University Press, 1971), pp. 78-89.

16. M. M. Bakhtin, *The Dialogic Imagination: Four Essays*, ed. Michael Holquist, trans. Caryl Emerson and Michael Holquist (Austin: University of Texas Press, 1981), p. 255.

17. Emir Rodríguez Monegal, "The Metamorphoses of Caliban," *Diacritics* (September 1977): 78-83. Rodríguez Monegal also examines the impact of Bakhtin on Latin American authors and critics in his "Carnaval Antropofagia Parodia," *Revista Iberoamericana* 108-9 (July-December 1979): 401-12.

18. Roberto Fernández Retamar, *Calibán* (Mexico: Editorial Diógenes, 1970).

19. See my "Borges the *Criollo:* 1923-1932," *Review 28* (January-April 1981): 65-68.

20. I refer to the essay "De lo real maravilloso americano," first published as a preface to *El reino de este mundo* and later, in an expanded form, included in the collection of essays *Tientos y diferencias* (1964). For a description of Spengler's influence on Alejo Carpentier, see Roberto González Echevarría, *The Pilgrim at Home* (Ithaca: Cornell University Press, 1977), esp. pp. 55-57. A more detailed analysis of the influence of Spengler on Carpentier, including a description of the French Spenglerian Pierre Mabille, appears in Irlemar Chiampi's *O Realismo Maravilhoso: Forma e Ideologia no Romance Hispano-Americano* (São Paulo: Editora Perspectiva, 1980), esp. pp. 31-39. A Spanish translation was published in 1983 by Monte Avila Editores, Caracas.

Chapter One

1. For information on the course of the Spanish Civil War in 1937, see Hugh Thomas, *The Spanish Civil War* (New York: Harper and Row, 1963). Of particular relevance are chapters 43 and 56, which study the fortunes of the Republic over the course of 1937.

2. W. H. Auden, *Spain* (Great Britain: Faber and Faber, 1937). All quotations are taken from this edition.

3. Pablo Neruda, *España en el corazón: himno a las glorias del pueblo en la guerra (1936-1937)* (Santiago de Chile: Ercilla, 1938). The second printing is quoted here and contains this note: "This book was begun in Madrid, 1936, and continued in Paris and at sea, 1937." (My trans.)

4. Opinions on the generic nature of *Spain* vary markedly: George T. Wright, *W. H. Auden* (New York: Twayne, 1967), Stanley Weintraub, *The Last Great Cause: The Intellectuals and the Spanish Civil War* (Boston: Weybright and Talley, 1968), and George W. Bahlke, *The Later Auden* (New Brunswick: Rutgers University Press, 1970) associate it with the elegiac tradition, while Samuel Hynes, *The Auden Generation: Literature and Politics in England in the 1930s* (Great Britain: The Bodley Head, 1976), says it cannot be classified.

5. Arthur Rimbaud, Letter to Paul Demeny, May 15, 1871, in *Oeuvres*, ed. Suzanne Bernard (Paris: Garnier, 1960), p. 346. The translation quoted here is by Oliver Bernard, *Rimbaud* (Great Britain: Penguin Books, 1966), p. 10.

6. A. Bartlett Giamatti, "Proteus Unbound: Some Versions of the Sea God in the Renaissance," in *The Disciplines of Criticism: Essays in Literary Theory, Interpretation, and History*, ed. P. Demetz, T. Greene, and L. Nelson, Jr. (New Haven: Yale University Press, 1968), pp. 437-75.

7. Leo Spitzer, "Interpretation of an Ode by Paul Claudel," *Linguistics and Literary History* (Princeton: Princeton University Press, 1967), pp. 193-236.

8. Frederick Buell, *W. H. Auden as Social Poet* (Ithaca: Cornell University Press, 1973).

9. Edward Mendelson, *Early Auden* (New York: The Viking Press, 1981), p. 316.

10. Justin Replogle, *Auden's Poetry* (Seattle: University of Washington Press, 1969), p. 44.

11. That Auden would no longer be able to commit himself to a political cause after his experiences in Spain is abundantly clear after a reading of *The Prolific and the Devourer*, "a book of aphorisms and reflections written in the summer—and abandoned in the autumn—of 1939. It reflects Auden's attitudes in his first months in America, at a moment of transition between his equivocal Marxism in the 1930s

and his committed Christianity in the 1940s and after." In Auden's own words, "The artist qua artist is no reformer. Slums, war, disease are part of his material, and as such he loves them. The writers who, like Hemingway and Malraux, really profited as writers from the Spanish Civil War, and were perhaps really of some practical use as well, had the time of their lives there." *The Prolific and the Devourer*, ed. Edward Mendelson, whose preface (n.p.) is quoted above, in *Antaeus* 42 (Summer 1981): 19.

12. See in this context Enrico Mario Santí's *Pablo Neruda: The Poetics of Prophecy* (Ithaca: Cornell University Press, 1982).

13. Paul H. Fry, *The Poet's Calling in the English Ode* (New Haven: Yale University Press, 1980), p.9.

14. See in this context Emir Rodríguez Monegal's *El viajero inmóvil: introducción a Pablo Neruda* (Buenos Aires: Losada, 1966).

15. Neruda's translations of Blake appear in *Cruz y raya: revista de afirmación y negación* 20 (Madrid, November 1934): 87-109. The translations are reprinted in vol. 3 of Neruda's *Obras completas* (Losada: Buenos Aires, 1973).

16. William Blake, *The Poetry and Prose of William Blake*, ed. David V. Erdman, commentary by Harold Bloom (Garden City: Doubleday, 1970), p. 255.

17. Harold Bloom, "William Blake: 'The Mental Traveller.'" *The Visionary Company* (Ithaca: Cornell University Press, 1971), p. 61.

18. Roy Campbell, *Flowering Rifle* (Great Britain: Longmans, Green, 1939).

19. Robert C. Elliott, *The Power of Satire: Magic, Ritual, Art* (Princeton: Princeton University Press, 1970).

20. Alain Sicard, *El pensamiento poético de Pablo Neruda* (Madrid: Editorial Gredos, 1981), pp. 261-62.

Chapter Two

1. Jorge Luis Borges, *"Absalom, Absalom,"* *Borges: A Reader. A Selection from the Writings of Jorge Luis Borges*, ed. Emir Rodríguez Monegal and Alastair Reid (New York: E. P. Dutton, 1981), p. 93.

2. Jorge Luis Borges, "Prologue to *The Invention of Morel*," (1940), in *Borges: A Reader*, pp. 122-24.

3. Jorge Luis Borges, "Narrative Art and Magic," in *Borges: A Reader*, pp. 34-38.

4. Jorge Luis Borges, "*The Wild Palms*," (1939), in *Borges: A Reader*, pp. 93-94.

5. Joseph Conrad, *Nostromo: A Tale of the Seaboard* (Great Britain: Penguin Books, 1967). All quotations are from this edition.

6. Eloise Knapp Hay, *The Political Novels of Joseph Conrad: A Critical Study* (Chicago: University of Chicago Press, 1963), p. 214.

7. F. R. Leavis, *The Great Tradition* (New York: Doubleday, 1954), p. 231.

8. Carpentier in *El recurso del método*, García Márquez in *Cien años de soledad*, and José Donoso in *Casa de campo*. All quotations from *Casa de campo (A House in the Country)*, are taken from the first edition (Barcelona: Seix Barral, 1978). All translations are mine.

9. José Avellanos's book certainly has a bizarre life (or half-life) within Conrad's novel, as Frederick R. Karl points out: "He [Conrad] actively deceived, saying that for the history of Costaguana he depended on the "History of Fifty Years of Misrule" by the late Don José Avellanos. Conrad's point is truly Borgean: inventing a book within his own book, he then uses his Author's Note to cite it as one of his principal sources. If he had to divulge anything, he would reveal only what he had borrowed from himself! He had, in fact, most definite sources for names, events, and places." This revelation appears in Karl's biography of Conrad, *Joseph Conrad: The Three Lives* (New York: Farrar, Straus and Giroux, 1979), p. 542. Karl's chapter on *Nostromo* explains Conrad's ambiguous politics as well as his complex loyalties: the Pole, the European, the professional sailor, the artist.

10. J. Hillis Miller, *Poets of Reality: Six Twentieth-Century Writers* (Cambridge: The Belknap Press of Harvard University Press, 1966), p. 6. Hillis Miller is discussing "Heart of Darkness" in the passage quoted, but his ideas apply as well to *Nostromo*.

11. Alan Sandison, *The Wheel of Empire: A Study of the*

Imperial Idea in Some Late Nineteenth and Early Twentieth-Century Fiction (London: Macmillan, 1967), p. 138.

12. Jocelyn Baines, *Joseph Conrad: A Critical Biography* (New York: McGraw-Hill, 1960), p. 301.

13. Karl Marx and Friedrich Engels, *Die heilige Familie, oder Kritik der Kritishen Kritik: gegen Bruno Bauer und Konsorten*, in *Werke*, vol. 2 (Berlin: Dietz Verlag, 1962), p. 37. (My trans.)

14. For a discussion of the relationship between Donoso's earlier work, *The Obscene Bird of Night*, and *Frankenstein*, see my *Modern Latin American Narratives: The Dreams of Reason* (Chicago: University of Chicago Press, 1977).

Chapter Three

1. Victor Brombert, *La prison romantique* (Paris: Librairie José Corti, 1975): "Rachat spirituel, mais aussi salut par l'imagination: liberté réprimée et invention son intimement liées. On comprend dés lors qui l'image du poéte séquestré fascine: le Tasse en prison n'a cessé de faire rever d'autres poétes. C'est que le lieu clos se conçoit aussi comme le lieu de la creation artistique" (p. 19). Prison as the scene of writing is a venerable idea: We need think only of Boethius.

2. William Godwin, *Caleb Williams*, ed. David McCracken (London: Oxford University Press, 1970). All quotations are taken from this edition.

3. Reinaldo Arenas, *El mundo alucinante* (Mexico: Editorial Diógenes, 1969). A translation of Arenas's text has been published under the title *Hallucinations*, but it is long out of print. I have translated all quotations.

4. Jorge Luis Borges, "Prólogo" in Adolfo Bioy Casares, *La invención de Morel* (Buenos Aires: Emecé, 1968), p. 12: "La novela característica, 'psicológica,' propende a ser informe. . . .Esa libertad plena acaba por equivaler al pleno desorden. Por otra parte, la novela 'psicológica' quiere ser también novela 'realista': prefiere que olvidemos su carácter de artificio verbal y hace de toda vana precisión (o de toda lánquida vaguedad) un nuevo toque verosímil. . . . La novela de aventuras, en cambio, no se propone como una transcripción de la realidad: es un objeto artificial que no sufre

ninguna parte injustificada." (The typical "psychological" novel tends to be formless. . . . That complete freedom ends up being the same as complete disorder. In addition, the "psychological" novel also aspires to be a "realist" novel: It wants us to forget its being verbal artifice and makes all useless precision (all languid vagueness) into a new true-to-life touch. . . . The adventure novel, on the other hand, does not present itself as a transcription of reality: It is an artificial object that tolerates no unjustified element.) (My trans.) This text is included in *Borges: A Reader.*

5. Northrop Frye, *The Secular Scripture: A Study of Romance* (Cambridge: Harvard University Press, 1976), p. 15: "Romance is the structural core of all fiction: being directly descended from folktale, it brings us closer than any other aspect of literature to the sense of fiction, considered as a whole, as the epic of the creature, man's vision of his own life as a quest."

6. Jorge Luis Borges, "Partial Magic of the *Quijote*," *Other Inquisitions* (Buenos Aires: Emecé, 1960), pp. 68-69: "Why does the fact that don Quijote is a reader of the *Quijote* or Hamlet a spectator of *Hamlet* disturb us? I think I know why: Such inversions suggest that if the characters in a fiction can be readers or spectators, we, their readers or spectators, can also be fictitious." (My trans.)

7. This phenomenon reappears in *Frankenstein*, by Godwin's daughter Mary Shelley, when Frankenstein decides to take charge of his own story, rather than have his benefactor do it for him. so that the version released in the world be whole and not "mutilated." This idea of a story as personal property is also an important subject in José Donoso's *A House in the Country* (see above, chap. 2, pp. 82-87).

8. See Edward W. Said, *Beginnings: Intention and Method* (New York: Basic Books, 1975), p. 16: "Every sort of writing establishes explicit and implicit rules of pertinence for itself: certain things are admissible, certain others are not. I call these rules of pertinence *authority*—both in the sense of explicit law and guiding force (what we usually mean by the term) and in the sense of that implicit power to generate another word that will *belong to* the writing as a whole (Vico's etymology is *auctor*: *autos*: *suis ipsius*: *propsius*: property)."

9. Miguel de Cervantes, *The Life and Exploits of Don Quixote de la Mancha*, trans. Charles Jarvis (London: Jones and Co., 1831), p. 7.

10. Virginia Woolf, *Orlando* (New York: Harcourt, Brace, 1928), pp. 14-15.

11. Maria di Battista, *Virginia Woolf's Major Novels: The Fables of Anon* (New Haven: Yale University Press, 1980), p. 17. The passage Professor di Battista quotes is from Woolf's *A Room of One's Own*.

12. In this context, see the essay by Claudio Guillén mentioned above in the introduction. Guillén reviews Cervantes's attack on the first-person narrative: "Genre and Countergenre," pp. 154-58.

13. Jonathan Culler, "Apostrophe," *The Pursuit of Signs: Semiotics, Literature, Deconstruction* (Ithaca: Cornell University Press, 1981), p. 142: "One who successfully invokes nature is one to whom nature might, in turn, speak. He makes himself a poet, visionary. Thus invocation is a figure of vocation."

14. Jorge Luis Borges, "Kafka y sus precursores," *Otras inquisiciones* (Buenos aires: Emecé, 1960), pp. 147-48. (My trans.)

15. For a discussion of this idea in Balzac's writings, see F. W. J. Hemmings, *Balzac: An Interpretation of La Comédie Humaine* (New York: Random House, 1967), pp. 8-18.

Chapter Four

1. Georg Wilhelm Friedrich Hegel, *Estetica*, ed. and trans. Nicolao Merker and Niccola Vaccaro (Milan: Giulio Einaudi Editore, 1967); see esp. p. 1223.

2. Georg Lukács, *The Theory of the Novel*, trans. Anna Bostock (London: Merlin Press, 1971); see esp. the section "Integrated Civilisations."

3. Northrop Frye, *The Great Code: The Bible and Literature* (New York: Harcourt Brace Jovanovich, 1982), p. 224.

4. Aristotle, *Poetics*, trans. Gerald F. Else (Ann Arbor: University of Michigan Press, 1967), pp.21-22.

5. On invective in poetry, see above, p.54.

6. Martin Gardiner, ed. *The Annotated Snark* (New York: Simon and Schuster, 1962). See also below, note 10.

7. Jorge Luis Borges, "Tlön, Uqbar, Orbis Tertius," *Ficciones (1935-1944)* (Buenos Aires: Emecé Editores, 1967). Two studies on this story were especially useful to me: James E. Irby, "Borges and the Idea of Utopia," *Books Abroad* (Summer 1971): 411-20; and Emir Rodríguez Monegal, *Jorge Luis Borges: a Literary Biography* (New York: E. P. Dutton, 1978).

8. I wish to thank Professor James C. Nohrnberg of the University of Virginia for generously sharing his unpublished research on Milton's epics with me.

9. Martin Gardiner, ed. *The Annotated Alice: Alice's Adventures in Wonderland and Through the Looking Glass* (New York: Bramhall House, 1960).

10. Jean Gattégno, *Lewis Carroll: Fragments of a Lookingglass*, trans. Rosemary Sheed (New York: Thomas Y. Crowell, 1976), p. 10. Other works that illuminated this aspect of Lewis Carroll are: Robert Martin Adams, *Nil: Episodes in the Literary Void During the Nineteenth Century* (New York: Oxford University Press, 1970); Edward Guilano, ed. *Lewis Carroll Observed: A Collection of Unpublished Photographs, Drawings, Poetry, and New Essays* (New York: Clarkson N. Potter, 1976). See esp. Harold Beaver. "Whale or Boojum: an Agony," pp. 116-27.

11. There are actually two "first editions" of "Tlön, Uqbar, Orbis Tertius," one that appeared in the magazine *Sur*, no. 68 (May 1940); and another in the *Antología de la literatura fantástica*, ed. Adolfo Bioy Casares, Silvina Ocampo, and Jorge Luis Borges (Buenos Aires: Editorial Sudamericana, 1940). There are minor textual differences between the two versions, most importantly the narrator's first statement in the postscript: "I reproduce the preceding article just as it appeared in Number 68 of *Sur*—jade green covers, May, 1940". The reader, of course, is holding that very issue in his hands and experiences a kind of play within-a-play *frisson*. The versions available in English derive from the one Borges republished in *Ficciones* (1944), which reproduces the text in the anthology of fantastic literature, where the postscript alludes to the anthology instead of *Sur*.

12. *Prólogo,' La vida de Lazarillo de Tormes*, ed. Everett

W. Hesse and Harry F. Williams (Madison: University of Wisconsin Press, 1969), p. 8.

13. Jorge Luis Borges, "La biblioteca total," *Sur*, no. 59 (1939): 16. This essay is the intellectual precursor of the tale "The Library of Babel" and appears in English as "The Total Libarary," in *Borges: a Reader.*

14. Jorge Luis Borges, "El tintorero enmascarado Hákim de Merv," *Historia universal de la infamia* (1935) (Buenos Aires: Emecé Editores, 1967), p. 97. The stories in *A Universal History of Infamy* have been translated into English by Borges and Norman Thomas di Giovanni. The English version is actually a conceptual rewriting of the original, quite different in style.

15. Severo Sarduy, "Escritura Travestismo," *Escrito sobre un cuerpo* (Buenos Aires: Editorial Sudamericana, 1969), p. 45.

16. Jorge Luis Borges, "Profesión de fe literaria," *El tamaño de mi esperanza* (Buenos Aires: Editorial Proa, 1926), pp. 146-47.

17. Simon Wilkins, ed. *Sir Thomas Browne's Works*, vol. 3, "Hydriotaphia: Urn Burial; or, a Discourse on the Sepulchral Urns lately Found in Norfolk" (1658) (London: William Pickering, 1835), p. 490.

Chapter Five

1. Thomas Carlyle, *The French Revolution: A History* (New York: Modern Library, 1934), p. 167.

2. Richard Garnett, *Life of Thomas Carlyle* (London: Walter Scott, 1887), pp. 177-78.

3. Hayden White, *Metahistory: The Historical Imagination in Nineteenth-Century Europe* (Baltimore: The Johns Hopkins University Press, 1973), p. 148.

4. Thomas Carlyle, "The Hero as Poet," *On Heroes, Hero-Worship and the Heroic in History* (London: Oxford University Press, 1928), p. 111.

5. Thomas Carlyle, "On History," *Critical and Miscellaneous Essays* (Boston: Phillips, Sampson and Co., 1858), p. 221.

6. Philip Rosenberg, *The Seventh Hero: Thomas Carlyle*

and the Theory of Radical Activism (Cambridge: Harvard University Press, 1974), p. 76

7. Thomas Hardy, *The Dynasts: An Epic-Drama of the War with Napoleon in Three Parts, Nineteen Acts, and One Hundred and Thirty Scenes* (New York: St. Martin's Press, 1977), p. xxvi.

8. R. J. White, *Thomas Hardy and History* (London: Macmillan, 1974), p. 19.

9. Florence Emily Hardy, *The Life of Thomas Hardy, 1840-1928* (New York: St. Martin's Press, 1962), p. 334.

10. Walter F. Wright, *The Shaping of The Dynasts: A Study in Thomas Hardy* (Lincoln: University of Nebraska Press, 1967); see esp. pp. 44-53.

11. Euclides da Cunha, *Os Sertões* in vol. 2 of *Obra Completa*, ed. Afrânio Coutinho (Rio de Janeiro: José Aguilar Editöra, 1966). Translated by Samuel Putnam as *Rebellion in the Backlands* (Chicago: University of Chicago Press, 1970), p. 89. All quotations are taken from this edition.

12. Thomas Carlyle, "Dr. Francia," *Critical and Miscellaneous Essays* (Boston: Phillips, Sampson and Co., 1858), p. 547.

13. Mario Vargas Llosa, *La guerra del fin del mundo* (Barcelona: Plaza y Janés, 1981). The book has been translated as *The War of the End of the World*. Page references are to the original edition; all translations are mine.

14. Joseph Frank, "Spatial Form in Modern Literature," *The Widening Gyre* (New Brunswick: Rutgers University Press, 1963).

15. Robert B. Cunninghame Graham, *A Brazilian Mystic, Being the Life and Miracles of Antonio Conselheiro* (New York: Books for Libraries Press, 1971).

Bibliography of Works Cited

Adams, Robert Martin. *Nil: Episodes in the Literary Void During the Nineteenth Century*. New York: Oxford University Press, 1970.

Arenas, Reinaldo. *El mundo alucinante*. Mexico: Editorial Diógenes, 1969.

Aristotle. *Poetics*, trans. Gerald F. Else. Ann Arbor: University of Michigan Press, 1967.

Auden, W. H. *The Prolific and the Devourer*, ed. and pref. Edward Mendelson. *Antaeus* 42 (Summer, 1981).

———. *Spain*. Great Britain: Faber and Faber, 1937.

Bahlke, George W. *The Later Auden*. New Brunswick: Rutgers University Press, 1970.

Baines, Jocelyn. *Joseph Conrad: A Critical Biography*. New York: McGraw-Hill, 1960.

Bakhtin, Mikhail. *The Dialogic Imagination: Four Essays*, ed. Michael Holquist, trans. Caryl Emerson and Michael Holquist. Austin: University of Texas Press, 1981.

———. *Problems of Dostoevsky's Poetics*. ed. and trans. Caryl Emerson, intro. Wayne C. Booth. Theory and History of Literature, vol. 8. Minneapolis: University of Minnesota Press, 1984.

Benjamin, Walter. *Reflections: Essays, Aphorisms, Autobiographical Writings*, ed. and intro. Peter Demetz, trans. Edmund Jephcott. New York: Harcourt Brace Jovanovich, 1979.

Blake, William. *The Poetry and Prose of William Blake*, ed. David V. Erdman, commentary by Harold Bloom. Garden City: Doubleday, 1970.

Bloom, Harold. *The Anxiety of Influence: A Theory of Poetry.* New York: Oxford University Press, 1973.

———. *The Visionary Company.* Ithaca: Cornell University Press, 1971.

Borges, Jorge Luis. "La biblioteca total." *Sur* 59 (1939).

———. "El tintorero enmascarado Hákim de Merv," *Historia universal de la infamia.* Buenos Aires: Emecé Editores, 1967.

———. "Kafka y sus precursores," *Otras inquisiciones.* Buenos Aires: Emecé Editores, 1960.

———. "Magias parciales del *Quijote*," *Otras inquisiciones.* Buenos Aires: Emecé Editores, 1960

———. "Profesión de fe literaria," *El tamaño de mi esperanza.* Buenos Aires: Editorial Proa, 1926.

———. Prologue to *La invención de Morel* by Adolfo Bioy Casares. Buenos Aires: Emecé Editores, 1968.

———. "Tlön, Uqbar, Orbis Tertius," *Ficciones (1935-1944).* Buenos Aires: Emecé Editores, 1967.

———. *Borges: A Reader*, ed. Emir Rodríguez Monegal and Alastair Reid. New York: E. P. Dutton, 1983.

Brombert, Victor. *La Prison Romantique.* Paris: Librairie José Corti, 1975.

Buell, Frederick. *W. H. Auden as Social Poet.* Ithaca: Cornell University Press, 1973.

Campbell, Roy. *Flowering Rifle.* London: Longmans, Green, 1939.

Carlyle, Thomas. *Critical and Miscellaneous Essays.* Boston: Phillips, Sampson and Co., 1858.

———. *The French Revolution.* New York: Modern Library, 1934.

———. *On Heroes, Hero-Worship and the Heroic in History.* London: Oxford University Press, 1928.

Carroll, Lewis. *The Annotated Alice: Alice's Adventures in Wonderland and Through the Looking-Glass*, ed. Martin Gardiner. New York: Bramhall House, 1960.

———. *The Annotated Snark*, ed. Martin Gardiner. New York: Simon and Schuster, 1962.

Cervantes, Miguel de. *The Life and Exploits of Don Quixote de la Mancha*, trans. Charles Jarvis. London: Jones and Co., 1831.

Chiampi, Irlemar. *O Realismo Maravilhoso: Forma e Ideologia no Romance Hispano-Americano.* São Paulo: Editora Perspectiva, 1980.

Conrad, Joseph. *Nostromo: A Tale of the Seaboard.* Great Britain: Penguin Books, 1967.

Cortázar, Julio. *Rayuela.* Buenos Aires: Editorial Sudamericana, 1963.

Culler, Jonathan. *The Pursuit of Signs: Semiotics, Literature, Deconstruction.* Ithaca: Cornell University Press, 1981.

da Cunha, Euclides. *Os Sertões,* ed. Afrânio Coutinho. In vol. 2 of *Obra Completa.* Rio de Janeiro: José Aguilar Editôra, 1966.

Cunninghame Graham, Robert B. *A Brazilian Mystic, Being the Life and Miracles of Antonio Conselheiro.* New York: Books for Libraries Press, 1971.

Curtius, Ernst Robert. "Spain's Cultural Belatedness." In *European Literature and the Latin Middle Ages,* trans. W. Trask, New York: Harper and Row, 1963.

di Battista, Maria. *Virginia Woolf's Major Novels: The Fables of Anon.* New Haven: Yale University Press, 1980.

Donoso, José. *Casa de Campo.* Barcelona: Seix Barral, 1978.

Elliott, Robert C. *The Power of Satire: Magic, Ritual, Art.* Princeton: Princeton University Press, 1970.

Fernández Retamar, Roberto. *Calibán.* Mexico: Editorial Diógenes, 1970.

Frank, Joseph. *The Widening Gyre.* New Brunswick: Rutgers University Press, 1963.

Frye, Northrop. *Anatomy of Criticism: Four Essays.* Princeton: Princeton University Press, 1957.

———. *The Great Code: The Bible and Literature.* New York: Harcourt Brace Jovanovich, 1982.

———. *The Secular Scripture: A Study of Romance.* Cambridge: Harvard University Press, 1976.

Fry, Paul H. *The Poet's Calling in the English Ode.* New Haven: Yale University Press, 1980.

Fuentes, Carlos. Interview: "The Art of Fiction, LXVIII." *The Paris Review* 82 (Winter 1981).

García Márquez, Gabriel. *Cien años de soledad.* Buenos Aires: Editorial Sudamericana, 1967.

Garnett, Richard. *Life of Thomas Carlyle*. London: Walter Scott, 1887.

Gattégno, Jean. *Lewis Carroll: Fragments of a Looking-glass*, trans. Rosemary Sheed. New York: Thomas Y. Crowell, 1976.

Giamatti, A. Bartlett, "Proteus Unbound: Some Versions of the Sea God in the Renaissance." In *The Disciplines of Criticism: Essays in Literary Theory, Interpretation, and History*, ed. P. Demetz, T. Greene, and L. Nelson, Jr. New Haven: Yale University Press, 1968.

Gledson, John. *The Deceptive Realism of Machado de Assis: A Dissenting Interpretation of 'Dom Casmorro.'* Liverpool Monographs in Hispanic Studies 3. Liverpool: Francis Cairns, 1984.

Godwin, William. *Caleb Williams*, ed. David McCracken. London: Oxford University Press, 1970.

Guiliano, Edward, ed. *Lewis Carroll Observed: A Collection of Unpublished Photographs, Drawings, Poetry, and New Essays*. New York: Clarkson N. Potter, 1976.

Gledson, John. *The Deceptive Realism of Machado de Assis: A Dissenting Interpretation of "Dom Casmurro."* Liverpool Monographs in Hispanic Studies, 3. Liverpool: Francis Cairns, 1984.

González Echevarría, Roberto. *The Pilgrim at Home*. Ithaca: Cornell University Press, 1977.

Guillén, Claudio, "Genre and Countergenre." *Literature as System: Essays Toward the Theory of Literary History*. Princeton: Princeton University Press, 1970.

Hardy, Florence Emily. *The Life of Thomas Hardy, 1840-1928*. New York: St. Martin's Press, 1962.

Hardy, Thomas. *The Dynasts: An Epic-Drama of the War with Napoleon in Three Parts, Nineteen Acts, and One Hundred and Thirty Scenes*. New York: St. Martin's Press, 1977.

Hartman, Geoffrey H. *Beyond Formalism: Literary Essays, 1958-1970*. New Haven: Yale University Press, 1971.

Hay, Eloise Knapp. *The Political Novels of Joseph Conrad: A Critical Study*. Chicago: University of Chicago Press, 1963.

Hegel. Georg Wilhelm Friedrich. *Estetica*, ed. and trans. Nicolao Merker and Niccola Vaccaro. Milan: Giulio Einaudi Editore, 1967.

Hemmings, F. W. J. *Balzac: An Interpretation of La Comédie Humaine.* New York: Random House, 1967.

Hesse, Everett W., and Williams, Harry F., eds. *La vida de Lazarillo de Tormes.* Madison: University of Wisconsin Press, 1969.

Hillis Miller, J. *Poets of Reality: Six Twentieth-Century Writers.* Cambridge: Belknap Press of Harvard University Press. 1966.

Hirsch, *Validity in Interpretation.* New Haven: Yale University Press, 1971.

Hynes, Samuel. *The Auden Generation: Literature and Politics in England in the 1930s.* Great Britain: Bodley Head, 1976.

Irby, James E. "Borges and the Idea of Utopia." *Books Abroad* (Summer 1971).

Iser, Wolfgang. *The Act of Reading: A Theory of Aesthetic Response.* Baltimore: Johns Hopkins University Press, 1978.

Jauss, Hans Robert, "Literary History as a Challenge to Literary Theory." *New Literary History* 3 (Autumn 1970).

———. *Aesthetic Experience and Literary Hermeneutics,* trans. Michael Shaw, intro. Wlad Godzich. Theory and History of Literature, vol 3. Minneapolis: University of Minnesota Press, 1982.

Karl, Frederick R. *Joseph Conrad: The Three Lives.* New York: Farrar, Straus and Giroux, 1979.

Leavis, F. R. *The Great Tradition.* New York: Doubleday, 1954.

Lukács, Georg. *The Theory of the Novel,* trans. Anna Bostock. London: Merlin Press, 1971.

Mac Adam, Alfred J. "Borges the *Criollo*: 1923-1932," *Review 28* (January-April, 1981).

———. *Modern Latin American Narratives: The Dreams of Reason.* Chicago: University of Chicago Press, 1977.

Marx, Karl, and Engels, Friedrich. *Die heilege Familie, odes Kritik der Kritishen Kritik: gegen Bruno Bauer und Konsorten.* In *Werke,* vol. 2. Berlin: Dietz Verlag, 1962.

Mendelson, Edward. *Early Auden.* New York: Viking Press, 1981.

Neruda, Pablo. *España en el corazón: himno a las glorias del pueblo en la querra (1936-1937).* Santiago de Chile: Ercilla, 1938.

Replogle, Justin. *Auden's Poetry.* Seattle: University of Washington Press, 1969.

Rimbaud, Arthur. Letter to Paul Demeny, May 15, 1871. *Oeuvres.* ed. Suzanne Bernard. Paris: Garnier, 1960.

Rimbaud. Great Britain: Penguin Books, 1966.

Rodríguez Monegal, Emir. *El Boom de la novela latinoamericana.* Caracas: Editorial Tiempo Nuevo, 1972.

———. "The Boom: a Retrospective." Interview with Rodríguez Monegal, *Review 33* (September-December, 1984).

———. "Carnaval/Antropofagia/Parodia." *Revista Iberoamericana,* nos. 108-9 (July-December, 1979).

———. *Jorge Luis Borges: A Literary Biography.* New York: E. P. Dutton, 1978.

———. "The Metamorphoses of Caliban." *Diacritics* (September 1977.

———. *El viajero inmóvil: introducción a Pablo Neruda.* Buenos Aires: Losada, 1966.

Rosenberg, Philip. *The Seventh Hero: Thomas Carlyle and the Theory of Radical Activism.* Cambridge: Harvard University Press, 1974.

Said, Edward W. *Beginnings: Intention and Method.* New York: Basic Books, 1975.

Sandison, Alan. *The Wheel of Empire: A Study of the Imperial Idea in Some Late Nineteenth and Early Twentieth-Century Fiction.* London: Macmillan, 1967.

Santí, Enrico Mario. *Pablo Neruda: The Poetics of Prophecy.* Ithaca: Cornell University Press, 1982.

Sarduy, Severo. *Escrito sobre un cuerpo.* Buenos Aires: Editorial Sudamericana, 1969.

Shelley, Mary. *Frankenstein or, The Modern Prometheus.* Afterword by Harold Bloom. New York: New American Library, 1965.

Sicard, Alain. *El pensamiento poético de Pablo Neruda.* Madrid: Editorial Gredos, 1981.

Spitzer, Leo, "Interpretation of an Ode by Paul Claudel." *Lin-*

guistics and Literary History. Princeton: Princeton University Press, 1967.

Thomas, Hugh. *The Spanish Civil War.* New York: Harper and Row, 1963.

Thomson, Clive. "Bakhtin's "Theory" of Genre." In *Studies in 20th Century Literature* 9, no. 1. Special Issue on Mikhail Bakhtin, ed. Clive Thomson (Fall 1984).

Vargas Llosa, Mario. *La guerra del fin del mundo.* Barcelona: Plaza y Janés, 1981.

Vidal, Hernán. *Literatura hispanoamericana e ideología liberal: surgimiento y crisis (una problemática sobre la dependencia en torno a la narrativa del Boom).* Buenos Aires: Ediciones Hispamérica, 1976.

Weintraub, Stanley. *The Last Great Cause: The Intellectuals and the Spanish Civil War.* Boston: Weybright and Talley, 1968.

Wellek, René, and Warren, Austin. *Theory of Literature.* Third ed. New York: Harcourt, Brace and World, 1962.

White, Hayden. *Metahistory: The Historical Imagination in Nineteenth Century Europe.* Baltimore: Johns Hopkins University Press, 1973.

Wilkins, Simon, ed. *Sir Thomas Browne's Works.* London: William Pickering, 1835.

Woolf, Virginia. *Orlando.* New York: Harcourt, Brace, 1928.

Wright, George T. *W. H. Auden.* New York: Twayne, 1967.

Wright, Walter F. *The Shaping of the Dynasts: A Study in Thomas Hardy.* Lincoln: University of Nebraska Press, 1967.

Index

Index